Beyond the Finish Line

Dream big &
follow your heart.

[signature]

Library and Archives Canada Cataloguing in Publication

Guloien, Krista, 1980-, author
    Beyond the finish line : what happens when the endorphins
fade / Krista Guloien.

Issued in print and electronic formats.
ISBN 978-1-77141-169-1 (paperback).--ISBN 978-1-77141-170-7
(pdf)

    1. Guloien, Krista, 1980-. 2. Rowers--Canada--Biography.
3. Athletes--Retirement. 4. Athletes--Retirement--Psychological
aspects. I. Title.

GV790.92.G85A3 2016   797.12'3092   C2016-902710-4   C2016-902711-2

Beyond the Finish Line

What Happens When the Endorphins Fade

Krista Guloien

First Published in Canada 2016 by Influence Publishing

Book Cover Design: Marla Thompson
Book Cover Photo: Marla Guloien
Editor: Nina Shoroplova
Proofreader: Sue Kehoe
Typeset: Greg Salisbury
Portrait Photographer: Natalia Anja, www.nataliaanja.com

I dedicate my book to my family who has always stood by me not only as I pursued the Olympic dream, but always.

You don't choose your family, but if I had that option I would choose the exact same people. My mom, dad, and sisters are the foundation and compass that guide me.

Thank you Mom for always believing that I can achieve anything, including writing this book. It was you who first believed in the story I had to tell.

Thank you Dad for being a safe place where I could bounce around ideas without judgment. Your feedback through my writing process was more valuable than you know.

Thank you Leah for knowing me so well. You always understand how I am feeling and where I am coming from. You assume the best in me and I feel stronger knowing that you have my back.

Thank you Marla for always being the rock star that you are. You are my baby sister, but I often look up to you. I am constantly inspired by your relentless pursuit of your dreams. Thank you for all of your helpful feedback and input.

My love for all of you has no bounds.

Testimonials

"Krista tells her story of strength and vulnerability from the inside out. Anyone can imagine the competitive battles Olympians face during their career, but Krista gives readers a glimpse of what we Olympians try hard not to reveal: our post sport struggles. Transition is scary. As she works to redefine herself after an Olympic medal, Krista shares her journey of reflection and introspection; what sport gave to her; and what she had to give to it.

"I found her honesty—as she tries to reconcile her aggressive, confident Olympian-self with her more introverted just-me-self— to be not just refreshing but incredibly healthy. Olympic athletes all feel the nausea that accompanies transitioning from sport; taking our 'Olympian me' and learning how to apply it somewhere new. Krista's Beyond the Finish Line *will resonate with anyone who finds that it's time to move from one passion to another."*

Marnie McBean, O.C.
Three-time Olympic Rowing Champion

"Krista sheds the spotlight on the highly competitive and stressful world of Olympic athletes, a world where you compete with your best friend for the last seat in the boat, a world where the difference between winning and losing can be measured in fractions of a second. She takes us from the elation of winning an Olympic medal to the roller coaster ride of transition to life after sport. This is not just a book about sport: it is about a woman's journey to discover who she is, what is most important in her life, and how she can contribute; this is a journey we can all relate to."
Silken Laumann, Olympian, Inspirational Speaker, and Author of *Unsinkable: A Memoir,* **Silken & Co Productions Ltd., www.silkenlaumann.com**

"Olympians are rare creatures. Each is capable of extraordinary things.

"In a poignant and truthful way, Krista Guloien reveals that every Olympian is an ordinary person who struggles to succeed in life's journey long after the race is over."

Scott Russell, Commentator/Host CBC Sports

Acknowledgements

My family: my parents, Dawna and Nels Guloien, and my sisters Leah and Marla Guloien, you are my motivation. Your support during this process—either through the creation and editing or simply listening when I struggled—was more appreciated than you probably know. Grandma Verna and Grandpa George Williams, Grandma Margaret and Grandpa Paul Guloien, you are the foundation that our family is built upon and I thank you for raising such amazing people to become my parents.

My crew at the London Olympics: Ashley Brzozowicz, Carolyn Ganes, Darcy Marquardt Hortness, Natalie Mastracci, Andréanne Morin, Cristy Nurse, Janine Stephens (née Hanson), Lesley Thompson-Willie, Rachelle Viinberg, N.D. (née DeJong), and Lauren Wilkinson, the strength you exemplified gave me strength I never knew I had.

My coaches from 2001-13: Michelle Darvill, Carsten Hassing, John Keogh, Al Morrow, Volker Nolte, Ph.D., Craig Pond, and Allison Ray, your leadership showed me the way. I am very thankful for the time and effort you sent my way.

Thank you to all the people who have helped me along the way, in my life, in my sport career, and beyond; I am forever grateful for your love and support. Also, to everyone who helped to make this book become a reality. Finally, to my publishing team at Influence Publishing, who helped me establish the structure and schedule I needed to bring this book to life.

In life, as in sport, no success is achieved in solitude. It truly does take a team. I am forever grateful to all the different teams I have been lucky to be a part of.

I must also acknowledge my two dogs, Charlie and Arthur. They will never read this, but I want to share that although they have helped me procrastinate more than anything, they always make me smile inside and out. I love them as unconditionally as they love me. We may not have a long time together, but we sure are having a good time.

Contents

Dedication v

Testimonials vii

Acknowledgements ix

Introduction xiii

Chapter 1: Being Selected to Row in London 1

Chapter 2: The Build-Up 11

Chapter 3: The Preparation, the Plan, and the Execution on Eton Dorney 21

Chapter 4: The Mindset of an Olympian 35

Chapter 5: Beyond the Sport 45

Chapter 6: Homecoming: From Hero to Zero 57

Chapter 7: A Love Life outside Sport 65

Chapter 8: Self-Belief over Doubt 71

Chapter 9: Struggling with Congratulations 75

Chapter 10: Post-Traumatic Body Image 83

Chapter 11: Saying Goodbye to My Sport 89

Chapter 12: Adjusting to Post-Olympic Life 97

Chapter 13: You Are Enough 101

Chapter 14: Life after Rowing 105

Chapter 15: My Mom, My Strength, My Perspective 111

Chapter 16: My First Half Marathon 117

Chapter 17: Leaving One Opportunity to Find Another 125

Chapter 18: Training the Mind to Be Present 129

Chapter 19: Glass Half Empty or Glass Half Full? 137

Chapter 20: Fitness and Pressure 141

Chapter 21: A Career after Rowing 149

Chapter 22: Transferable Skills: The Legacy Sport Leaves Behind 155

Chapter 23: Building a Tribe 161

Chapter 24: Transition Like a Champion 165

Appendix: Quotable Quotes..175
Author Biography...181
Professional Speaker..183

Introduction

It is now 2016 and I have been retired from full-time sport since April 2013, leaving my sport on a high after winning a silver medal for Canada in rowing women's eights. In some ways, I feel like I left that life a long time ago. In other ways, it feels as though I am just on an extended break from the life I lived so intensely for so long. My sport career was a once-in-a-lifetime journey, filled with ups and downs. Physically and emotionally, I was tested beyond anything I could have imagined. That is until I retired and was faced with the challenge of rebranding myself and figuring out what to focus my time and energy on next.

Racing creates a physiological dose of endorphins, which numb the pain and induce a euphoric state that fades fast beyond the finish line. Following my sport career, my life has been filled with ups and downs that have led me to immense personal growth and progress. I have realized that the struggle of working outside my comfort zone is really where the magic happens. I don't always welcome it, but I have never looked back and thought it wasn't worth it for some reason or another. I have now started to seek challenges in my everyday life. Telling this story is part of my journey beyond the finish line.

> Meeting new people and making connections have been critical to my development, especially as I work to rebrand myself and try to find my way

Recently, I attended an event to announce to the media that the Americas Master Games were to be held in Vancouver. My thought and intention was that I would go and make some good connections, as well as support a local sporting event. Ironically, it launched me into an unexpected emotional tailspin. Firstly, mingling and networking with strangers is not my forte, but it is a great skill to have. Meeting new people and making connections have been critical to my development, especially as I work to rebrand myself and try to find my way. Even if I feel shy, I put myself into the networking scenario at least once per month, if not weekly. This was a great opportunity and I had a great conversation with another former Olympian. It was relatable and constructive, but it brought up emotional baggage that I had clearly been suppressing.

An hour and a half later, I was driving away feeling an overwhelming sense of anxiety. I was panic-stricken, with an elevated heart rate and a racing mind thinking about all the work I still had to do in order to figure out my life and future. I was being bombarded by fear.

While I have been working on many different projects, I have not been making a steady income. Financial validation and security was not something I experienced in my career on Canada's women's rowing team. I was happy to leave a low-income lifestyle behind. Unfortunately, it has taken me a lot longer than I would have imagined to create the stability I crave. Experiences, like the one I had at this media event, instigated insecurities and questions, and I got myself wound up to a place where I felt like I was going to vomit with emotion.

Luckily, my sister Marla was at my house when I got home and she reminded me that she could relate to everything that I was saying. I was not alone.

I am in a mad panic and rush to get to this place where I feel I'll be deemed successful, but what does success look like? Why do I not feel successful yet? Perhaps as an athlete, I am addicted to lofty goals and big achievements and nothing is ever going to be enough. Without the next dangling carrot in my sights, I am lost. In many ways, my Olympic success haunts me. How will I ever top it?

I am not satisfied if I am not reaching for something hard or challenging. I am driven by the deep-seated drive to achieve. It is not an option to be complacent. The pressure I put on myself is exhausting and I know there are other people out there struggling and doing this to themselves as well. At times, being in my own head is so overwhelming that it makes me want to go home and lie in bed with my dogs rather than face the world.

> Will I be able to speak to large groups of people and sound like a genuine version of myself?

Writing a book became my dangling carrot. I pursued writing this story, my story, in the hopes of unmasking the somewhat-taboo topic of athletes and their immense struggle after retiring from a career in sport. Writing a book, teaching spin, and public speaking in an effort to help others through my experiences are now my new pursuits.

My internal dialogue is not always positive or supportive of my quest. I am wondering if I am a good-enough writer. Will I be able to speak to large groups of people and sound like a genuine version of myself? Will I be able to work through the nerves that will inevitably come from putting myself out there? Do I have to do a lot of networking in order to get speaking engagements? I hate networking. That further begs the question of whether I am pursuing what I should be pursuing. Will I love what I do when my career gets up and running? Do I even like writing and speaking to large groups? My mind is busy non-stop.

It is hard for my support system to help me answer these personal questions, because the answers ultimately need to be answered by me and me alone. I sometimes wish that someone could just tell me what to do. With my marching orders, I could confidently go in the direction I am instructed; but that is not the way it works. If that were the case, I would probably hate that too. I want to metaphorically write my life story and be in control, but in fear I realize I am in a vulnerable place from which to operate. It is an unsure place where it is tough to direct energy effectively.

In life, there is no pathway that does not include self-doubt, overanalysis, self-critique, low moments, feeling overwhelmed, and questions of whether we should quit and move on. It is all part of the quest to be better. Most of us forget these benchmark moments when we are on the other side. I forgot that I had them when I was rowing, but I did.

In one of my panic-stricken conversations with my sister when I was downloading all my worries to her, she needed to remind me that I had had moments like these when I was rowing as well. She looked at me in shock when I said I didn't remember them. I don't remember either feeling that doubtful of what I was pursuing or of myself, I told her.

With her assistance, I realized that I have constructed a story with my memories, almost like a fairy tale. I recalled that I never questioned if rowing was what I should be pursuing. It sounds so good, doesn't it? But I was fooling myself and she called me out for it.

As she remembers it, I would call home at least once or twice a month crying and questioning what I was doing. As memories started to come out of the woodwork for me, I started to recall what she was saying. It was surreal for me that I somehow had repressed this part of my rowing journey. I did have low moments. I did call and question what the heck I was doing. "Do I have what it takes? Does the coach believe in me? Am I going fast enough to make the team? Would everything I've sacrificed and all of the hard work pay off or am I going to be coming home with nothing?"

It was so hard on some days that I didn't think I would be able to push through. It was strange to me that it literally took my sister to call me out and remind me of all the tearful phone calls I'd made to her, as well as to the rest of my family, about my fears and worries before I remembered having any in my rowing journey.

> We all doubt ourselves and only we can choose how we respond to our doubts.

We willingly take a risk in hanging on to our dreams despite the outcome. In the low moments our worries will plague us, but only briefly. I wonder if I used to call my sister to release these feelings so that I could let them go. Perhaps that is why I don't remember them. It is healthy and necessary to crack and be vulnerable with someone we are comfortable with. I think it is important to admit our thoughts and feelings so we can go forward and move on.

I never did anything but move forward as a rower despite feeling like I didn't know what might happen around the next turn. It is not like I ever did anything with these doubts and these questions. I was never going to pack up and walk away. It was always a risk that I wouldn't make the team and not go to the Olympics, but quitting wasn't an option.

I feel no differently about my quest for success as an author and a speaker now.

Inspirational clips and motivational quotes conjure the belief that successful people are exempt from self-doubt and internal conflict. WRONG! We all doubt ourselves and only we can choose how we respond to our doubts. Do we push on, do we back down, or do we avoid this experience altogether by never starting?

How is it that I thought my past in rowing was exempt from these struggles? In transition I have lost myself. I forget what it was like to pursue something from the start and my expectation is that I want success now, not in time, but RIGHT NOW. In my darkest moments I am horribly impatient and panicked about where my life is taking me.

The day after my meltdown, I felt better and more at peace. It was ironic because nothing had changed. It became a valid lesson that even when we feel like everything is falling apart, chances are everything is not falling apart and the feelings will pass. With time and some mental clarity, we feel better.

Three days after my networking meltdown, I felt a wave of acceptance and appreciation for all that I have. I am hard on myself, arguably too hard on myself. I realize that on my worst days, I am dwelling on what I am missing in my life and not on all that is good.

On that Friday, as I rode my bike with my other sister, Leah, I realized that I am in a unique point in my life. I have a great family that has been emotionally and financially supportive of my transition from sport and it is all going to work out. It may take more time than I want, but transition is a process much like the process of becoming an Olympic rower, which took me many years. It is important to remember the process when we are feeling a panicked sense of rush toward wherever we are headed. We need to know that these feelings are heightened in the moment and the panic will pass. When we are focusing on what we don't have, a simple tweak in our perspective could take us to thoughts of what we do have.

I have written this book to share what I learned from my journey as an Olympic athlete, but just as important is what I have learned in my time after my career concluded as a full-time athlete training for the Olympics. Although there have been many times I was convinced I was the only one struggling through my transition from sport, I know that is not the case. If I can help one person to feel comfortable in their transition, maybe even laugh at the awkwardness and tackle one of the many new challenges coming their way, then I have succeeded!

Photo By: Mike Murray

Chapter 1

Being Selected to Row in London

There was one final round of selection leading up to the London 2012 Summer Olympics. This would end up being for my seat in Canada's women's eight rowing team. We were months out from the games and it came down to a race between me and one of my teammates. Two of us would compete for one seat. A handful of races over two days would determine the fate of my every hope and dream. All the training, previous selections, and countless races at home and away came together in those final moments. Either I would make it or I wouldn't.

I had made every national team from 2006, but I almost didn't make the London 2012 team. From the outside, it would have seemed that I obviously would be there, but behind the walls of the training centre, I was fighting tooth and nail. It is cruel and unusual because although we appear at lead-up events (for example, the send-off dinner in Toronto) and take team photos, we don't even know if we are going anywhere but home with a broken heart. We are literally walking on eggshells.

It is not a given, as nothing is, but I got a very heightened sense of this when I was trying to make the 2012 Olympic team. The pool of candidates to represent Canada in the women's eight was small, and the margin of difference between one rower and the next was minimal—mere seconds. When it came down to it, we really had nine athletes for eight seats. You would think that makes for pretty good odds, but it didn't feel that way when I knew I could be the one of nine with no seat. Just because something has happened before does not predict what will happen in the future and the pre-Olympic selection time in London, Ontario was the scariest time of my life, not the most exciting as some might think. That is the beauty and beast of sport—the switch can flip at any moment and that switch can be in your favour or not.

In the world of rowing, it is commonplace to spend ninety percent of the time fighting to rank yourself and secure your spot. Coaches capitalize on the internal competition. We were always on our toes and fighting for our spot. What this meant for us was that we never really knew where we stood. Personal factors, such as injury or illness, were somewhat more challenging to control and were additional wild card factors beyond my influence and outside of racing against my teammates. The ultimate question was, would my body withstand all the training and allow me to move forward and be in contention for a spot? I saw many an athlete and teammate leave the centre with broken dreams for this reason. Nothing was a given and no one was safe.

My final selection races were to make sure that I was the right candidate for the eight and to see if there was more power and spark to uncover in our crew. As a result, we also found more power and spark in me as an athlete.

In rowing, as in many endeavours such as other sports, writing books, and in the public speaking world, balancing rivalry between colleagues is challenging. We are pinned up against one another, measured and compared with one another. The same teammates that I would eventually race with in the crew comprised some of my fiercest competition at home. An odd contradiction to balance while in training and selection, as I had to look out for number one selfishly, but selflessly be ready to battle as a crew in the Women's Eight.

For the most part, it's good healthy competition, which in sport also helps athletes to raise their game and stay accountable. It can, however, put a fair amount of tension on inter-team relationships. For London, I was going up against one of the newer and younger members of our team. She was someone whom I had grown to respect and care about. She was like a little sister to me. Racing to achieve my dream was the goal, but it was hard for that to be at the cost of hers. Getting through those two days of racing felt like torture and the waiting time to hear the final result seemed like an eternity.

It couldn't have been more awkward and tense around the boathouse, as my remaining teammates and training partners tried their best to stay objective and unbiased toward the situation. Although the other rowers involved were not directly racing for their seats, they were meant to race as hard as they could for each piece as if their spot were on the line too. Yet, we all knew that everyone had an opinion. In a boat with eight other individuals, can a single individual really be measured? I am not sure, but I had to buy in. I chose to surrender and trust that we all had enough respect for one another that we would never throw a race for one person to win over the other. Can you truly separate your consciousness from your unconsciousness in such a situation? It is hard to find a measure for the data and statistics when it comes to heart.

Not only did I have two days of the most physically intense racing I had ever had, but also there was an emotional component as my Olympic opportunity was at stake. I had come to the most challenging crossroads of my entire career. If I didn't win my spot, would I be okay?

I have a great family; I have my health and many great things in my life outside rowing. Regardless, I couldn't wrap my head around not winning. The other side of the fence was absolutely unbearable for me to even imagine. It sent me into a state of panic; not only because of what I was about to go through, but because I knew that my mind was in an unhealthy mental state. This is when I decided to reach out to our sport psychologist, Kirsten Barnes … as I'd done before when I felt like I needed her to help me with my mental performance. I basically had to call out that I was broken mentally and I needed her to set me straight quickly.

Kirsten comes from a highly successful Olympic rowing background, so she knew what I was about to go through from personal experience. Her perspective and advice calmed me down and got me into a more positive frame of mind. It all came back to focusing on the process and not the bigger picture. I could only control the moment I was in, so I decided I might as well be in it a hundred percent and give it all that I had. Beyond that, the chips would fall where they may.

A select few of my teammates reached out to me in a respectful way during this time. They simply acknowledged that they supported me and empathized. We had all been there at one time or another, as selection is a norm. It was nice to hear from them and I appreciated it immensely. However, I felt that one of my closest teammates, Janine, was steering clear of me. I started to narrate this crazy story in my mind that she didn't want me in the crew. I knew it wasn't true, but it got in my head, so I reached out to her and let her know how I was feeling and told her that I was really struggling. It ended up being her advice that anchored me the most. She told me to write a list of the reasons why I would make the boat and leave the list beside my bed. She had done this herself when she had a low point earlier in the quadrennial (a time period of four years and the time in between one Olympics and the next). She said to leave it there and read it when I woke up or at any time I needed a little pick-me-up. She emphasized that it was important for me to be fuelled by where I had come from and all that I had accomplished.

This is what I wrote:

I deserve to be in the boat.

I have improved from the last season to now.

I am rowing well and have been easy to coach.

I help to motivate others.

I am aggressive and can race hard.

My stroke is long and efficient.

I am going to do this.

I am going to win here at home, so I can win while I am away.

I have been through many scenarios like this.

I am going to do this!

On the morning of the selection races, I was more charged up and ready to go than I had ever been. No one would know the result before the racing was complete and the data was calculated. Sitting on the line of my first piece, which was the 1,100 metres (m) in the eight, it never felt like a fight between the two of us as one might think. She was far from my enemy, but rather a teammate whom I loved and respected. It was about the dream, and I was willing to drop the gloves and go to the ends of the earth to fulfill my plan. I had done the work and I was ready to put it all on the line, and I did. The spark of energy and boat speed I felt when the eight took off in those first strokes put me at ease and gave me confidence. There was no way that this boat could have gone any faster with anyone else in it.

I brought all of my passion, will, drive, and grit to the races that day on our home lake in London, Ontario. My teammate Darcy said she knew I had it in me to win when I yelled out "Go, Canada" before one of our selection races. Funnily, I don't remember saying a word. I only remember the first hundred metres of the first race.

There would end up being a total of eight races of different lengths over two days, in order to average out the results and provide the judges with enough data: four 1,100 m races and four 500 m races. Half of the races were in the eight-person crew and the other half in a two-person crew (a pair). This is called a seat-racing matrix in rowing. It is a bit of a gong show, but it is the way it's done.

Looking casual, we sat quietly floating in position until we were called to start. My mind, however, did not recognize this situation as casual. This was my chance for an Olympic performance so I could be chosen to compete in the Olympics. Nothing less than a world-class performance would be good enough to win.

On go, there was a charge and a surge in the boat speed that I knew could not be beaten. Leading up to this moment, I had worried if there was such a thing as going too hard and ruining the race, but my body knew what to do. That first stroke calmed me. As an individual, this race was about being selected for

Canada's women's rowing eight, but for the team, the goal was to make the fastest possible eight for Canada at the Olympics. No matter how much it might seem as though one person was on the chopping block, the goal in rowing any crew boat is to make a fast crew, never a fast individual rower. I took comfort in the fact that I was part of something bigger than myself. The spot was mine for the taking and I knew that I was the better candidate for the job.

> Leading up to this moment, I had worried if there was such a thing as going too hard and ruining the race, but my body knew what to do. That first stroke calmed me.

We waited two long days while our coaches deliberated over the results and I finally got the news that my results had solidified my spot. As solid as it ever would be, at least. Two world cups were between then and the Olympics—one in Lucerne and one in Munich—and our performance at those would determine whether or not our line-up needed further evaluation. Later than most would likely expect, it would then be only four months until we would be competing at the Summer Olympics. No success was ever taken for granted. I was not about to let that seat slip out of my hands though. It was time to focus on racing and winning!

I am not the fastest rower as an individual, but I did prove myself in selection. I showed that I made that crew fast. I won my spot in the crew and I could now breathe easily and mentally prepare for the biggest race of our careers.

I wasn't without sadness though for my rowing sister who now had her Olympic dream take on a new vision, as she would now become the spare. Unknown to us at the time, however, our Olympic crew would need her services as a spare when we had a crewmate's injury affect her ability to participate at one hundred percent, and so in the end my selection challenger raced in the London Olympic women's eight and she got herself a silver medal too! What a cyclone of events.

There was no excitement at the training centre, as when one person is selected another is not and we all had the utmost respect for each other. The only considerate place for me to celebrate was with my family, so I called and announced my spot was "secure." Saying it out loud for the first time felt like the first time even though I had been on the Canadian team to Beijing Summer Olympics in 2008. What a relief! I was going to the Olympics again! I spoke with my mom first. We cried happily and finally let ourselves be excited for what was to come in London, Great Britain.

For my family, I am sure it was a breath of fresh air to hear I had made the team. It was also a serious relief, as the trip to London was planned well before I was officially named to the team and I had been calling home daily worried that I wasn't going to make it. My family had spent a lot of money and made plans so they would be able to support me from the grandstands before I even had my seat. My poor mom and dad must have been stressing, but they never let me know it. Calling home was always one of the first things I did when there was any news—even though most of our news came at 8 a.m. (Eastern Standard Time, EST) and they were on the West Coast of Canada where it was three hours earlier at 5 a.m. (Pacific Standard Time, PST). I woke them up many times over my career and especially during that week of racing for my spot.

Gaining my seat in Canada's Olympic crew was the pinnacle

moment of my rowing career up to that point and debatably it was the hardest challenge. Racing at home with my heart and soul on the line got me ready and hungry for the Olympic stage. In the next phase, I would be stepping out onto that world stage with my crew to show what we Canadians are made of.

Chapter 2
The Build-Up

You rehearse, you discuss, and you imagine everything up until the moment you cross the finish line. Of course, you need to imagine and believe that the podium and winning gold can be yours, but to actually go there is like going to a mythical place in your mind. Near the end of the journey when this dream was closer to becoming a reality in 2012, I avoided thinking about it in an effort to resist jinxing my team and myself. For me, it was important to stay in the moment, focus on the present experience, and avoid fixating on what we were there to do in London.

Without ever saying it, we all knew what we were there to do as we had lived and breathed the dream of Olympic gold more intensely than we ever had since crossing the finish line last at the Beijing Olympics in 2008. Coming eighth out of eight crews in the women's quad in Beijing had been my wake-up call. If I was going to stay around I knew two things to be certain. For a start, I wanted to be the best and secondly, I knew I could do more to get there. It was then that a fire was re-ignited.

The Olympic experience is more than just the races and competition between opening and closing ceremonies. The Olympic voyage really began for me the moment I was officially named to the team and I was able to say out loud that I would be representing our sport and our country. The feelings of pride that I got and the excitement to live my dream, as well as to be a part of something bigger than myself and my sport, kicked off in a real way at that point.

The Olympics are an enormous production. The athletes and the sports are only one part of it. Taking in the Olympic Games as an organizer, or as a spectator and fan are completely different experiences than what we as athletes experience. Parents and friends were actually coached by Rowing Canada to make sure they didn't include us in too many of the logistics as it could cloud our heads and add additional stress that we quite frankly could not handle. I was thankful for their advice, as it is probably one of the hardest things to ignore your excited friends and family. These are the most important people to you and they have done so much for you, but they can be very distracting.

After my first games in Beijing, I referred to my Olympic experience as "being in the Olympic bubble." It is like living in a protected zone that you enter upon arrival at the airport. There are volunteers and media, everyone is dressed in Olympic gear and affiliated to a team of athletes or a country, and everyone has a job. There are separate customs lines for huge groups of countries and teams as they arrive. Our arrival in the host country was a well-orchestrated event in both Beijing and London, and something that I never expected to be operating so elaborately.

Once through customs with our bags, we were led out of the airport and through a swarm of media. It was fun to smile and wave in hopes that our families back home might see our arrival. This is the introduction to the rock-star status that athletes receive when they compete in the games. We, as athletes, were the stars of the show and people want to meet the athletes. It was just as exciting for me to meet the other athletes, as I am a big Olympic and sports fan myself.

I appreciated this part of the journey and role that we take on as Olympic athletes. The games are about the world coming together to share sport. We are ambassadors and leaders of the games and I take that very seriously.

We saw famous Chinese basketball player Yao Ming as we were heading to the CBC headquarters for an interview after racing was finished in London. We were so excited and running off a major high so we asked him for a picture. He was very focused and denied us, as he had to go to his practice. As he lumbered off, I promised myself I would try my best to never be like that because it was incredibly disappointing to get turned down by an athlete we looked up to. In his defence, he was in the zone and still focused on competing, so I don't hold it against him. "Don't be a Yao" is still a motto of mine though.

Outside the bubble, the Olympic village is bright and friendly and full of possibilities. Welcoming people, free swag, and free food are plentiful wherever you go. There are so many distractions you really have to keep your blinders on, as the last thing you want is an extra bag of M&M's to come in the way of you and your medal! By excluding as much stimuli from the outside world as we possibly could, there is a sense that within the bubble time starts to go in slow motion. It is like the movie *Groundhog Day* as we executed exactly the same routine daily, in the same surroundings, with the same small group of familiar faces.

People often wonder what it is like in the Olympic village. Who is sleeping with whom and did they really run out of condoms? Yep, that is the top question. It is impossible to escape "sex sells." No joke, it is probably the most popular question. I will go on record as saying I didn't see any of this behaviour until after the competitions were over. And what happens in the village stays in the village.

Leading up to our races, the Canadian rowers stayed outside the Olympic village to be closer to the racing course. We were in a small village called Slough, approximately five kilometres from Eton Dorney in a hotel that we essentially took over for the duration of our stay. Our coach, John Keogh, would drive us to and from the course up to three times per day.

> And what happens in the village stays in the village.

The goal of the week leading up to our final on August 2 was for nothing different to happen. It is at this point that nothing could make us faster by large margins, but there are numerous distractions, mishaps, and errors that could make us slower.

"The taper," as we call it, and "the tapered state" comprise an unfamiliar rested condition that we as athletes are completely unaccustomed to. It occurs when our body of work is done: the time leading up to Olympic racing is about harnessing the power that builds as the body recovers from the previous hours of training. Our time was completely dedicated to doing the fine-tuning and letting our bodies taper for the big day. There were only a few times per year when we would fully taper and compete at a hundred percent, not even during selection. It is a fine balancing act choreographed by the coaching staff. I wanted to be excited, alert, and relaxed, but not too excited, alert, and relaxed. I felt weird as the fog of training lifted. My senses started coming back.

> It is at this point that nothing could make us faster by large margins, but there are numerous distractions, mishaps, and errors that could make us slower.

I remember when one of my most noteworthy coaches Al Morrow, who had his first year as a National Team Coach the year I was born, used to tell us that as we started to taper we could start to feel things both physically and emotionally that we hadn't noticed before because we didn't have the mental energy to notice them until we'd had some rest. Like zombies coming to life, we had to take everything new we were feeling with a grain of salt and evaluate whether it was actually a new sensation that needed tending to or simply an increased awareness with newfound energy during the tapered state.

Over the days of taper and as the numbness and pain of the gruelling training became my past, this incredible level of physical and emotional energy started to build up within. This energy had to be controlled and stowed away to use at the right time when needed. This was where things could get a little dicey, as many athletes have made Olympic- and career-ending mistakes in the moments leading up to their race, likely attributed to this mental state. I was present, but in a different way. My presence existed for one thing and one thing only—an Olympic gold. At this time, only the Olympic bubble is safe. We avoided everything outside the necessary in order to stay protected.

> I was present, but in a different way. My presence existed for one thing and one thing only—an Olympic gold.

I knew there would come a time when all of this energy would come in handy. This is what made me so excited and so nervous all at the same time. We have all seen close finishes in sport, as in those 0.02 second finishes that we see in so many Olympic finals. The outstanding moments happen when athletes are fuelled by stowed emotion and energy and driven by heart and motivation to win. I guarantee that we would have a banned substance on our hands if we were able to bottle this energy and take it for an extra edge. I felt like I had superhuman strength, as though I was powered by an out-of-body source; debatably I was. It hurt with a mad fury, but I welcomed it and pushed towards it as the opportunity presented itself.

> The outstanding moments happen when athletes are fuelled by stowed emotion and energy and driven by heart and motivation to win.

In order to perfect a performance routine, we had executed countless rehearsals in many different genres. Back in Canada, we had rehearsed by having mock race days, selection races, local regattas, and national championships. Away from home, opportunities to rehearse and improve our abilities were at world cups and world championships, as well as at other international race opportunities leading up to the grand finale of the Olympics. The Olympics were and should be a place in our minds that we have been before, in every controllable way possible. That ultimately makes dealing with the additional Olympic stimuli much easier. My first national team world championship in 2006 was also in London, England, so for me I would be starting and finishing my high level rowing career in the same place.

Leading up to a big race, specifically the last few days, is the most peaceful part of the journey. The real work has been done and this was the calm before we got to show what we were made of. It was a bit like Christmas once all the presents are bought and wrapped because you really only ever got to see what you were capable of once per year: we only ever tapered this way for a big race. Every other time, we were training through our races and performances. From seeing our progress in a fatigued state, we knew how fast we were going, but now would be the time for us to actually show the world what we could do.

I knew without a shadow of a doubt that when push came to shove I would be able to deliver for my team and they would do the same. Our race motto was "hands in the fire" and to us this meant that when the race got intense and painful, we would all figuratively put our hands in the fire and hold them there with one another until we accomplished what we wanted. In my Olympic final, I could have stopped pulling when it hurt, but I would never let my team down. They brought out the best in me. Each of us relentlessly followed our mantra. We would not give up. We would have each other's backs through anything we had to face.

When I was in the zone, I was in a state of coiling and

building energy to go out there and fight against the teams that competing countries had produced. I became comfortable with having fear and nerves. Perhaps not comfortable, but saying "I embraced them" would be more accurate. They were something I had felt many times before.

My performance nerves resembled comical discomfort in the final moments leading up to one of my first real nerve-inducing races. That was the 36th World Rowing Championships in 2007 in Munich, Germany when I was rowing in a quad and we set out to qualify the event for the 2008 Beijing Summer Olympic Games. I remember sitting in my hotel room so filled with unendurable nerves that I felt like blasting through the hotel doors and running for the hills. I would have killed for my spot earlier in the season and now that I had it within my grasp I wanted to run. What sense did that make? How could I be so nervous for something I wanted so badly and had fought so hard to get? Recognizing this silly contradiction calmed me and grounded me in how special the moment was.

The days leading up to our 2012 Olympic race were a cycle of eating, rowing, massage, physiotherapy, and team meetings. For the last years of my crew days, my teammate Ashley Brzozowicz and I shared a hotel room and even that was rehearsed. We had a choreographed dance of sorts to keep our lives away from home easy and comfortable. I was always packing, organizing, or sleeping. The sleeping I termed "meditation," because sometimes I wasn't really sleeping, but rather I would be simply lying with my eyes closed under an eye mask. Weirdly, I found this most comforting. It was the only way I could relax my mind and stop myself from overthinking what we were there to do. Ashley, on the other hand, would read and read and read. It was no wonder she is so smart (she has a BA from Yale) as while I was lying on my bed sleeping or meditating as I cheekily called it, she was taking in information. For her, that was how she stayed relaxed and saved her energy. We clung to our somewhat boring routine as the days, hours, minutes, and seconds passed by, bringing us closer to our goal.

Leaving our hotel room for the last time was rather symbolic. Without saying anything, we knew that the next time we came back to our room we would be forever changed.

Photo By: Mike Murray

Chapter 3

The Preparation, the Plan, and the Execution on Eton Dorney

Eton Dorney, which is also known as Eton College Rowing Centre and as Dorney Lake, is a man-made rowing facility finished in 2006. It is near the village of Dorney, approximately three kilometres west of Windsor. When I reflect back on my time at Eton Dorney and on racing in the 2012 Summer Olympics in London, Great Britain, I think of the final race that took place on August 2, 2012 at 12:30 p.m. I forget that the racing actually began four days earlier, on July 29 at noon when we raced Romania and the Netherlands in the second of two heats.

I am going to explain how the heats or preliminary races shape the final race for six crews. There are seven qualified crews to race in the Women's Eight event at the Olympic Games. Two heats took place on July 29; ours was a heat among three countries and the other heat was among four. The countries that took first place on this day would proceed straight to the final on August 2 and the remaining crews would race again in a repechage on July 31. Having seven boats and only six lanes in any rowing race, including the final, means that through the *repechage* one boat would lose its Olympic hopes of a medal finale in London; as it turned out, Germany didn't make the cut.

Both the Canadian crew and the American crew won our heats to advance directly to the final on August 2. It was a physical and mental release and a relief to have that initial Olympic race under our belts. We were positioned right where we wanted to be and with this initial success we could go back to work with three full days to work on polishing up our final strategies. It was great preparation for the final race; even though it didn't lend itself to drawing any conclusions. The final would be a completely different ball game.

The challenging part of having won our heat was that after having had to get ourselves revved up to compete on the world stage, we then had to shift back down and hang on for a few more days before doing it again, this time for the podium.

Once the ball was rolling and we were there it really came down to making sure we didn't screw it up. We did this by keeping true to our routine, staying calm and collected as individuals, as well as with one another through a high-energy and emotional time, keeping any negative influences out, and using more sanitizer than I ever imagined possible.

Believe it or not, many athletes come down with a cold or get food poisoning before a big event. Catered food, shared spaces, being away from home, and unfamiliarity with everything can be the perfect recipe for a disaster. It is important to protect the work. As athletes, we put a lot of blood, sweat, and tears into our sports to have it all measured on one day, at one specific time, and in one place. There are no delays (unless mother earth decides she wants one); there are no second chances. There is more than enough that we cannot control, so we made sure we stayed on top of all that we could control.

> As athletes, we put a lot of blood, sweat, and tears into our sports to have it all measured on one day, at one specific time, and in one place.

Staying healthy away from home and at competition had become a common practice. Having travelled as a group over ten to twenty times per year, we had perfected our routines and had either imagined, experienced, and/or seen all of the less-than-ideal scenarios that could arise. With all that we learned, we created habits such as using hand sanitizer whenever we were exposed to anything. Although you might think that athletes would be some of the healthiest people on the planet, we can in fact become quite susceptible to germs when we are using all of our body's energy for speed rather than for immunity.

There are so many factors that we could control, but so many that we could not. The Canadian Olympic Committee held a conference for us five hundred days—a year and a half—before the games. I will call one of the exercises we did with Marnie McBean, a four-time Olympic medalist in rowing, the "what if" assignment. Simply put, you take some time as a team and as an individual to come up with anything and everything that you can imagine might happen during the games and decide in advance how you would handle that event. This would include everything from losing your passport, to a team member getting injured, to something happening to someone in your family. Preparing for "what if" is a high-performance tactic. When the stakes are high it is a best practice to get ready for anything. If tragedy strikes you are giving yourself the best possible chance of getting through whatever comes your way with all of the success you dreamed.

I will never forget when, at the Vancouver 2010 Winter Olympic Games, Canadian figure skater Joannie Rochette experienced the tragedy of her mother passing away just days before she would compete. Something like that is not only hard to imagine on any day, but to have it happen at the Olympics would be earth shattering. For her to find the strength to compete, let alone take a bronze medal is outstanding and is an exceptional example of the mental fortitude that it takes to be an Olympian. I never had to overcome that level of adversity and I am thankful. Joannie Rochette inspired me and she will always be an Olympic hero in my mind.

Fortunately for our crew, all of our "what if" scenarios were just that and in the days leading to our final race we were cruising along like a well-oiled machine. The day arrived and on the morning of August 2, 2012, it was time to deliver.

The night before every race we would sit down as a team and work back from our assigned race time to come up with a plan for the next day. It was similar to previous races we'd entered, but we would use the time as an opportunity to bring up every situational consideration and adaptation we could think of to prepare us best. We finished each meeting closing our eyes to listen to Lesley Thomson-Willie, our coxswain, going over a race simulation. She would take us through our race from the starting blocks right through to the finish line, in the lead, so that once we were on the water the next day, we had already won in our minds.

I have often been asked what the role of a coxswain is and if the position is important. A coxswain (pronounced "coc'sun" and often shortened to "cox") is a key and critical team member, despite the fact that she does not have an oar. She is the brain of the boat. She speaks to us over a microphone while looking in the direction we are travelling, opposite to the rowers who are going backwards. They are privy to information like where we are in the field as well as if a gust of wind is about to hit either side of the boat requiring a slight change in our hand levels. The cox also holds a rudder to steer the boat and keep it running straight in our lane. She sits facing the stroke seat rower who is responsible for setting the crew's rhythm. When each rower leans forward at the top of her stroke and her oar enters the water, the coxswain and the stroke seat rower are less than two feet apart. Lesley could see in our stroke, Andréanne Morin, what we were all experiencing and she could react and adapt accordingly. Imagine two people facing each other that closely, giving it their absolute all. Up there in the stern of the boat, it's an intimate, potentially spit-and-sweat-exchanging situation.

Our coxswain, Lesley, has one of the most calm and assertive voices I have ever heard; we trusted her and moved however and whenever she told us to. Her Olympic resume of coxing five crews to Olympic medals is impressive and we respected her results. More importantly, she had been there with us the whole way and we trusted her with everything we had. A quote about Lesley from the games that I will never forget is "If Lesley doesn't know something about rowing, it isn't worth knowing." We were in good hands and we were in it together.

It is in some ways surreal to finally wake up on the day. Like any pivotal life event we anticipate, it takes so much time and effort to get to it and then no matter how hard we try, it goes by way too fast. Knowing this, my goal was to try and enjoy the moments and to savour the experience.

We woke up at 6 a.m. for a short row and then we went back to our hotel to have something to eat and finish preparing. One of the keys to our preparation was to figuratively overturn any and all stones that we could to unlock any hidden opportunity for additional speed. By the Olympics, we had devised a finely tuned routine leading up to any race. It included everything from five minutes of high-intensity work two hours before our race time to optimize our ability to perform high-intensity sprinting, to choking back multiple shots of beet juice to help with oxygen uptake in the blood supplying our muscles. Try downing multiple vials of lemon-infused beet juice on a nervous stomach and then tell me how much you like beets. I still cringe three years later when I see them on a menu.

> Like any pivotal life event we anticipate, it takes so much time and effort to get to it and then no matter how hard we try, it goes by way too fast.

We returned to the course three to four hours pre-race to begin our on-site/on-land preparation with chiropractic and physiotherapy treatments and spinning on the bikes before setting off in our boat for on-water preparation, fifty-five minutes before our race time.

Before we left the dock and headed out for the on-the-water portion of our warm up, John Keogh, our coach, gave us his final words. This was his last chance to impart any of his thoughts and wisdom before he would have to set us free.

On the Olympic rowing course, there is a warm-up area that is separate from the race area, as races were taking place while we were warming up. On other non-Olympic courses there might be warm-up lanes running alongside the racecourse and in some cases this could be termed interference, as boats would disrupt the water; it is ideal to have a confined and separate space to prepare.

From under an overhead foot bridge about two hundred metres from the docks we entered the warm-up area. Family, friends, and fans are not allowed in the boat bay and dock area, but they may stand along the footpath and behind the grandstands to see competitors in the warm-up zone. This would be the first time we would hear and see our family members and get one last hoot and hooray before they would see us finishing in the last 500 m stretch. It was a goose-bump-inducing moment to hear a familiar voice shouting encouraging words, like "go get'em, Canada," as we headed into the zone. This is such a charged and exciting time. I have yet to experience any feeling like that one when the nine of us set out to warm up for the Olympic final, cheered and supported by what felt like all of Canada.

We had never been so sharp, so energized, so rested, and so ready to lay it on the line; without saying it aloud, we were all in the same place, as if we were one.

Rowing is one of those sports that appears so calm and beautiful from the outside, but it is actually more screaming mad than tranquil inside. There is a lot going on.

Once we were warm and ready to go and after the race before us had cleared from the starting area, it was time to corral in the base of the warm-up area and be directed under another footbridge and onto the course. These minutes are the most intense non-racing times I have ever experienced. Imagine being pumped and ready to go and then you have to sit, wait, and slowly move into position. I felt like a caged bull waiting for the gate to drop, but I had to sit calmly and prettily, more like a swan.

> Rowing is one of those sports that appears so calm and beautiful from the outside, but it is actually more screaming mad than tranquil inside.

The starting gates at Eton Dorney consist of a person at the stern of the boat holding our crew in place, while at the bow a sturdy plastic slipper of sorts, referred to as "a boot," rises out of the water for our bow to sit in. This boot does the job of holding all six boats aligned and drops when the race begins. In the rowing world, this was the crème de la crème of starting zones.

It is the cox's job to sort out the plan of action during these final minutes. Lesley gave commands and made the most efficient choices to get us into the start gates as quickly and easily as possible. With a slight crosswind blowing, it was important for the rowers in the bow, including me in the third seat from bow, to communicate and lightly to tap our blades in the water so as to hold a solid starting position. We aimed to be as straight as an arrow pointing at the finish line two thousand metres away.

We had a tradition that Lesley would lead at the five-minute mark. She would call out each minute and lead us in focusing mentally on something that would set us up for a great start. Five minutes beforehand, we were to focus on all the training we had done leading up to this moment; at four minutes, we would focus on all the gains and successes we had made that season; at three minutes, we would focus on the crisp sharp rhythm we executed in the warm-up zone, picturing how we would repeat it in the body of the race; at two minutes, we would focus in on moving strongly and fast through our build into the finish; and in the final minute, we would focus and visualize our first stroke where we would pick up the boat, get it moving, and set the tone.

We would all travel down this funnel of time using mental recall and focused visualization to bring us into the moment, as well as to unite us mentally right down to the very first detail of what would become the launching pad of our race.

The starting area was a quiet, yet tense place where we could hear only the movements of other crews and the quiet chatter of officials and coxswains. Coxes who spoke English would whisper into the microphones, as anything that was said in English would most likely be shared with all countries; coxes speaking other languages were less likely to whisper.

The starting official's loudspeaker crackled and a monotone voice announced "one minute until start"; that was our cue to be sitting ready. He then counted out which country was in which lane: "Lane 1: Australia; Lane 2: Netherlands; Lane 3: United States; Lane 4: Canada; Lane 5: Romania; and Lane 6: Great Britain. Attention." All eyes were on Andréanne as she paid close attention to the light system, which closely mimicked a traffic light, except it only had red and green. The red would be lit and within seconds of the final country being announced, it switched to green, the boot would drop, and the games began!

Being in the lead was something that we never grew to expect, as you can never expect anything in rowing and it does not matter much as it does not determine where crews will finish a 2,000 m race. We did, however, experience a pattern of getting out of the start quickly and it was not unheard of to still be leading even going into the halfway mark. Regardless of where we stood at five hundred metres into a race, we went about *our* race plan and shifted into the rhythm and power that we had trained to produce; we were confident we would produce results.

Back at home, we had worked hard to make sure we would be able to keep pushing and moving faster through the second half of the race and particularly in the last five hundred metres. This was to match the strength of the Americans, as with their size and power, although they weren't usually fast to start, they had typically been able to row through any lead we had ever been able to produce in the past.

Lesley's voice was a lot calmer than the voice in my head that seemed to almost be yelling over her voice and instructions, but I could hear her and I trusted her with all that I had. It was all about pushing to the edge, but maintaining composure. It's a bit of a gamble, but you are trained to take it. It is controlled chaos through training your body and mind to go to the edge.

On August 2, 2012, it was definitely apparent that we were taking inches in those last five hundred metres, but for whatever reason our start did not get us out in front as it had in the past. Sitting in third position behind the United States and the Netherlands through the first 500 m mark, it was critical that we continue to pull ahead. No race was ever just against the undefeated Americans, as the Dutch, British, Romanian, and Australian crews were also on the medal hunt. The first thousand metres of an Olympic race are much like other races. Water, a lane, and other boats to race is all pretty standard. There is nothing fancy or particularly Olympic in the first half, so that is to say there was nothing in particular that made me feel the magnitude of the Olympic experience. This was a good thing. It was business as usual. No need to be aware of the enormity of the situation.

The scale of the race became increasingly apparent as we

approached the second half of the race and the grandstands. I couldn't hear anything specific, but it is like entering a tunnel of noise and energy. There is no crowd like an Olympic crowd for rowing. It felt like a blink in time. My body was in excruciating pain, but I couldn't feel it. My mind was thinking, hearing, and processing, but it was all a blur.

I recall one moment in the last five hundred metres when I could see a blur of orange off our port side. The Dutch! In that moment, I got an extra rush of power and energy to help protect us from any attacks.

In the last hundred metres, I was outside of myself. The rush of stimuli flooding my body was so intense that my ability to acknowledge anything I might be feeling was gone. All I remember is Lesley's voice telling us we were moving and noise. It is what we trained for. We trained so that we would be able to continue rowing with boat-moving precision to the very last stroke regardless of the circumstances. My body knew exactly what to do.

Six minutes and twelve point six seconds after that boot dropped, we were able to call ourselves silver medalists at the 2012 Summer Olympic Games. The USA team was in the gold medal position with 6:10.59 and the Netherlands with 6:13.12 went home with the bronze.

It was an overwhelming, dreamlike, and proud moment combined with relief to have accomplished what we set out to do. Yet it was also disappointing that we didn't take the gold, something we had wanted and never had. We were proven to have a fast start time, time and again in our races preceding the Olympics. But we did not get an early lead in our Olympic final and as the race unfolded it seemed we were never able to make up the distance that the Americans got on us early in the race. Despite having trained our finish to match the

Americans' final push and power, we just seemed to run out of course before we caught them.

Ultimately, we leave it all out there, so no matter how it turns out we will have no regret. I didn't have one shred of regret at the London 2012 finish line. I was proud of my crew, what we had done, where we had come from, and the race we gave on that day. The disappointment was fleeting for me and when I think of that moment my heart fills with pride. I can hear the crowd, feel the warmth of my muscles, and see the bright lights of achievement all around us.

On paper, one might think that winning three silvers consecutively over the 2010 World Rowing Championships, the 2011 World Rowing Championships, and then the 2012 Summer Olympics would be anticlimactic, but in reality there is nothing anticlimactic about it. I can attest that in order to repeat any successful performance at the highest level, it takes a heck of a lot of hard work and concentration.

> I can attest that in order to repeat any successful performance at the highest level, it takes a heck of a lot of hard work and concentration.

We trained for gold, we visualized gold, and we went for it day in and day out. In order to get there, we tried new things and pushed our limits as individuals and as a crew. I am confident that had we trained to simply maintain the second place we had previously, we would have fallen to the back of the field or been knocked out of the running altogether. I was proud to execute the race we did on that day in August 2012.

Would it have been amazing to stand in the middle of the podium with a gold medal around my neck while listening to *our* national anthem? Heck, yes, it would have been! But it was pretty darn phenomenal to sport that silver as well and you can be sure that "O Canada!" was playing in my heart and my head while I looked out into a sea of red-and-white supporters, family members, and friends (referred to by themselves as "support-oars" rather than "supporters") who had come out to cheer for us. It is a moment that a dream couldn't even produce. It was real and it was amazing.

Photo By: Dawna Guloien

Chapter 4

The Mindset of an Olympian

I have a quote on my wall at home that states, "Sports do not build character. They reveal it." It was coined by renowned sports writer Heywood Hale Broun and esteemed basketball coach John Wooden. It is one of my favourites to this day because, for me, it speaks to the success I had after finding something in life that I was meant to do. I believe that immense strength and talent is within all of us and anything can bring out that talent. Some of us may choose our particular talent knowingly and others may find it by coincidence, fate, or chance.

I began rowing at twenty-one, which is older than many high-performance athletes. I believe that everything I did early on in life, pre-sports (specifically pre-rowing), shaped me into the athlete that I became, regardless of my late start. I didn't really know that I had any genetic gifts of endurance and strength. I did, however, seem to tower over others in height (a rowing advantage, I learned later), and I was always a passionate kid driven to get whatever I wanted.

Volleyball was my best sport in elementary through to high school, but I was never a star player. I put in the work and I had the drive to be a star player, but I was never able to get ahead of the plays and anticipate where I should be on the court. Regardless, sport made me feel strong and the court was a place where I was encouraged to take control and take initiative. Between the ages of ten and sixteen, I didn't feel I had a whole lot of control in the grand scheme of things. Sport made me feel free and empowered to push my limits.

School was something I was taught to value. I was driven to get top grades, as well as to compete in sport. I did some track and field, seasons of field hockey and volleyball, but I never really found a sport that I felt was mine. Volleyball came close, but because my ability to anticipate a play was seemingly not a natural-born skill, I was constantly running and diving all over the place. Or sitting on the bench. I wasn't exactly feeling that this was my destiny, or seeing any sign that volleyball (or any other sport) was my calling—not like it was when I found rowing. If nothing else, these formative times made me realize that the bench wasn't good enough for me. Looking back, I appreciate that these early skills of scholarly drive and ambition for the court versus the bench were the foundation on which I would build my Olympic success.

So how did I find rowing?

It was actually my younger sister Leah who discovered rowing and joined the team at Simon Fraser University (SFU) in Vancouver, British Columbia (BC). I am the oldest of three daughters. Leah came just sixteen months after me, and Marla, the youngest, came two years after Leah. Having sisters so close in age has been the greatest life blessing. We have supported and encouraged one another throughout each of our endeavours, as well as shared our opportunities and successes with one another. Both my sisters have achieved great success in their own rights: Leah went on from rowing to become a professional cyclist and coach, and Marla has built a music, fashion, and media production empire from scratch. This is a testament to the amazing support of our parents. They have always instilled in us that we are strong, capable women with no boundaries or limits to our potential.

As the oldest sister, I was a bit of a copycat when it came to rowing. Leah came home and said she was going to join the rowing team at SFU. At the time, I was still at nearby Douglas College working towards having enough credits to transfer to Simon Fraser. It was as though a light bulb went off for me. Suddenly, I was daydreaming about rowing being "my sport."

Leah's rowing stories intrigued me and I thought that I might not only enjoy it, but be built for it. I learned that rowers were typically tall. My whole life leading up to this point, I kind of loathed that being five foot ten made me stand out. I didn't love towering over people, so I was keen to find a purpose for it. Where could this height be a real asset in my life? In rowing, five foot ten is not even tall!

It was rather ironic that Leah started rowing before me, as she would be classified as short in the rowing world at five foot six. It is also ironic that although I have always referred to Leah as my Mini-Me, she has also been my bodyguard. Back in elementary school days, I struggled with separation anxiety from my mom. For my mom to get me out the door and to school for an entire day was a real struggle from kindergarten to grade five. She would literally ask my little peanut of a sister to find me (we are sixteen months apart, but at the time I was about a foot taller than her) on the playground at recess and at lunch to make sure that I was okay. Leah would tell my mom she didn't want to because her friends were scared of me. I was tall and looked older than I was, but inside I was a timid, shy, and anxious kid. It wasn't until grade five that I started to come out of my shell; it was a long process.

I had come a long way since elementary school, but I always stayed close to home and my family. I chose Douglas College and SFU—both local post-secondary options—so I could remain close to the nest. Who knew that a simple choice to sign up for a learn-to-row class could be the gentle nudge I needed to soar from the nest.

During my first week at SFU, all the school clubs (sport, pastime, and academic) put on displays to attract students. I took the bull by the horns and went on a hunt for the rowing booth to sign myself up for rowing. As I was wandering through the crowd, someone jumped out and asked me, "Do you want to row?" I was looking for rowing, but rowing found me as well. I had been noticed because I was tall, but this time it was to make a boat go fast, not just to point out that I was tall. I can still remember how excited I felt. It was as though I knew something great was about to happen.

It was literally within the first few rows that I started to dream.

It was as though a fire had been ignited the moment I sat in that Simon Fraser University novice eight and the first page of what I knew would become a long rowing story was written. It was 2001, so in my head I calculated that the 2004 Olympics would be a tight squeeze (to say the least). It is said that it takes 10,000 hours of practice to become an expert at something and although I didn't know that at the time, I instinctively knew that three years was likely too short a time to become an expert rower and compete on the world stage. I decided that 2008 would be the first Olympics I could realistically set my sights on, and so I did.

I laugh at myself now, because I really had no business thinking that far ahead. I didn't even know what I was doing and I had no clue what I had to do to get to the Olympics, but I had this feeling that I could. I had met "the one," in the sport sense.

The journey from my first learn-to-row class, which concluded with a 500 m race, to my Olympic final in London, a 2,000 m race, taught me so much about taking raw talent and becoming a great athlete with that talent.

> The journey from my first learn-to-row class to my Olympic final in London taught me so much about taking raw talent and becoming a great athlete with that talent.

Success in sport is a coming together of many skills and traits, some of which are undetectable in the traditional recruitment process. Desirable skills include drive, ability to adapt and listen to environmental cues, and self-belief. I myself would pass some of the tests and measurements they use early on nowadays to deem an athlete as having potential, but I would fail others. Some of my crewmates from London would also fail some of those tests. You could have all the physical gifts in the world and measure up to be the next shining star, but in the end you might never make use of that anticipated potential. My fear for the future is that if we put certain athletes on a pedestal and others below the standard before they have even learned to row or to love rowing enough to be inspired to try, we might squash their ability to dream beyond their predictable potential.

There is no statistic for heart or team chemistry. There is so much more to a great athlete than his or her stats, such as the mental ability to overcome adversity, adapt to an ever-changing environment, and cope with extremely high levels of physical and mental stress. In a team environment there is the additional ability to not only work with others, but to excel alongside them. Talent is one thing, but the inner fire and drive I had to have to put all the ingredients together is never something anyone measured, credited me for early on, or predicted.

> There is no statistic for heart or team chemistry. There is so much more to a great athlete than his or her stats.

I would assure any and every upcoming rower that my success was due to much more than just the physical ability to crank on an oar and row backwards. I'm not saying that physical prowess and athletic ability aren't great and formidable qualities. It is more to point out that in order to have success in sport, you must also have many other talents and skills. I had to want to crank on an oar and go backwards and furthermore be willing to do whatever it would take to go as fast as possible over and over and over again. Perhaps this makes me even crazier, but I loved it.

People often say that they know someone who *could have* gone to the Olympics, but for some reason, usually life and work related, they never got there. Sometimes they are speaking about themselves in these conversations. I always take offence to this because I find it undervalues the journey and contribution made by the very few athletes who actually make their way to the Olympics. Potential is not a good measure of outcome. It is the hard work, sacrifice, and heart that reveal the difference between those who can potentially do it and those who actually do it.

> I would assure any and every upcoming rower that my success was due to much more than just the physical ability to crank on an oar and row backwards.

In some ways it is like being in a very long season of *Survivor*. You must be able to endure day after day of gruelling physical and psychological training. You must educate yourself on how the body and mind work together. You need to be your number one advocate, and you need to speak up when something doesn't feel right. I saw far too many athletes lose out on opportunities because they pushed themselves in the wrong way, at the wrong time, and got injured. No coach, physiotherapist, chiropractor, or doctor can tell you how you feel. Following anyone else's orders blindly would not have helped me achieve my goals. I really listened to my body and analyzed how I was feeling. I would also listen to and respect the opinions of all the professionals who helped us.

> Potential is not a good measure of outcome.

Canada's rowing program grew and developed over the years I was there and I am sure it had come leaps and bounds from the early days as well. We were lucky that we had so many healthcare practitioners to choose from. We had a physiotherapist, a massage therapist, an osteopath, and a doctor all a phone call or an appointment away. I would work with them, and combine what they told me with how I felt in order to come up with a strategy that would best treat any ailment I was enduring.

It isn't about second-guessing everyone, but rather about hearing advice as well as listening to yourself and getting to know your body. This was the key for me to be able to not only protect my body from injury and survive the training, but also to excel. For instance, rib stress fractures are a common injury in rowing. Everyone's body is different, but I learned that if I caught the signs of a sore rib early enough, I could manage my body in a way that kept me on the water.

The mindset of an injured athlete is a whole other book, but I can attest that it was hard to tell my coaches and teammates I needed a day off when I felt like I needed it. I came from a coaching system where we were told rather than asked to do something, so it was challenging to stand up and ask for anything as an individual. For me, it was easier to lie low and ask for nothing than to have my coach disagree with me and thereby call attention to myself in the wrong way. It was always a fine balance of obeying them and listening to my own instincts. I marched along like an obedient soldier for the majority of the time, but I also listened to my own gut over anyone else's voice.

Standing up for what I thought was right for me was vital to my success. Taking time to rest and heal when I needed to ended up being the difference between one day off versus three months sitting out and losing my seat altogether. It is critical, as an Olympic athlete, to be your best ally and not your worst enemy.

Only you know if you need to take a breather and there is no shame in that. Coaches and support staff care about the athletes, but the world championships will come and go regardless of whether one athlete is able to be there or not; if you can't manage yourself, you simply get left behind.

Typically, the title of champion is given to the one who can push through adversity and insurmountable levels of pain, but that's a very simplified notion that inspires Hollywood films. In reality, it is not just the adversity and pain that a champion must endure. They are also artfully mindful, wily, aware of their physical and psychological being, and tactical. I wasn't able to anticipate a play in volleyball, but once I was a rower I was able to see multiple plays ahead.

> Typically, the title of champion is given to the one who can push through adversity and insurmountable levels of pain, but that's a very simplified notion that inspires Hollywood films.

"Olympian" is a title I will hold forever, but its meaning for me will change shape as I move on through life. I may be retired from competitive world-class sports, but I am still an Olympian. I thought life would be different after I achieved success at the Olympics. I thought Olympic success would transfer to every other area in my life. Unfortunately, it is a success that doesn't transfer. Not unless I do the work. The journey and transition beyond the finish line has tested me. It took time for me to realize that the skill set I developed as an athlete and the challenges I have endured have given me the power to transition like a champion and enjoy success in life beyond.

And so can you.

Photo By: Marla Guloien

Chapter 5

Beyond the Sport

I am so thankful that I had the gift of rowing and that I was able to do all that I did with my body. I am aware that without my physical health this would not have been an option and it is not something that I take for granted.

On the other hand, I do occasionally wish that I'd had something else earlier on that I loved in the way that I loved rowing. If I had spent as much time on whatever that might have been, I could then have carried on with that when rowing was over. I have heard a lot of advice given to athletes on this topic. Much of it makes complete sense. "Don't put all your eggs in one basket," and "your athletic career is only short term, so plan ahead."

It was not that I purposely ignored other passions, but I

didn't force them either. Rowing is and was all encompassing. It didn't leave enough mental or physical energy for much personal exploration. I also started rowing at twenty-one, in the midst of completing my bachelor's degree. I graduated with a B.A. in Criminology from Simon Fraser University in 2003 and then went into a full-on pursuit of being on the Canadian National Rowing Team. This required me to relocate from BC to London, Ontario. I went to immerse myself in rowing and surround myself with the best rowers in the country. I dropped the idea of building a career in criminology to go after the dream of competing at the Olympics.

Belief and Tenacity Go a Long Way

I moved out to London, Ontario bright eyed and bushy tailed, ready to do whatever it would take to make the National Rowing Team and compete for Canada. It was daunting, yet exciting to take this step in pursuit of my goals. Leaving my family was the hardest part.

At a rowing event much later, I was reminiscing about my career and prompted my first National Team coach Al Morrow to recall the first time he'd met me. It was a story that I held in the depths of my memory, but it came back to me in my reminiscent state. Unfortunately, he did not recall the event, which didn't shock me. He is a character who has had hundreds of athletes come through his program and, regardless of his not remembering it, this earlier moment in my career reminded me of my tenacity and the belief I had in myself even in the early days of my rowing journey. I'll tell it here.

It all began in the summer of 2004 when a handful of us from BC went out to London, Ontario to race in the national trials and train at the London Training Centre. We were preparing to go to Henley Regatta at Henley-on-Thames, England. This was a very pivotal opportunity in my development to travel internationally for a rowing competition. I was included as the token Simon Fraser University athlete in the boat as it was primarily initiated as a University of British Columbia and University of Victoria collaboration. I vividly remember being out for a row when someone said, "Look over there. That is the Olympic women's eight." We all stopped and ogled them from afar. I recall having so much admiration and excitement inside. I was as close to them as I had been to any real-life Olympians and they were rock stars to me. I had no idea how they were doing or what it truly meant to be in their shoes, but I wanted to know. Unfortunately, it ended up being the only time we crossed paths. It was like seeing a mythical creature at the end of the lake. They were only in town that morning and then they went off to Europe for further preparation leading up to the Athens Summer Olympic Games.

Back at the centre, tryouts were beginning for the 2004 non-Olympic world championships, which happen every Olympic year and include rowing races for events that are not part of the Olympic program, such as the heavyweight women's four and the lightweight women's quadruple sculls. We were all crowded into our billet's home late one morning after practice when Carola, one of my teammates and a really good friend, was called back to the centre. She was invited to take a swing at a non-Olympic world seat in a four-person boat for Canada. This was an exciting honour for her that meant the coaches saw her potential to give her this opportunity, especially so early in her career. I was envious of Carola, as I wanted more than anything to be in the same situation.

The offer was done in secret, which I had no idea would become the trend in rowing. I never truly knew what was going on or what would happen in the future. Later in my career, my teammates and I were careful not to assume anything, since inevitably, it would never go the way we thought. A great lesson I learned about life in general.

After days of angst and racing, Carola was named a non-travelling spare, which meant that she did not get to travel or race with the team, but would be called upon in the event that someone could not race for any reason. It was not quite what she wanted, but a benefit of this experience was that she became a "D-carded" athlete the following season. Being development carded meant she was now in the national team loop and would receive $500 per month from the government's Sport Canada training fund.

Obviously, the prestige of getting the D card is not about the money, but about being in the pool of national team athletes—an achievement in any rower's career.

After the racing season ended in September 2004, the new Olympics quadrennial began. Carola's next steps were to have a meeting with Canada's national rowing team head coach, Al Morrow. Carola was summoned to Victoria for this discussion and, given our very close friendship, I decided to accompany her. Additionally, I had plans to steal a moment with this messiah of rowing.

We took the ferry from Vancouver to Victoria and I set out to make it happen. This was to be my moment! I was lucky to seize the opportunity between time slots when someone didn't show up on time. I remember having to be spry and quick thinking to make it happen and not be too awkward about it, not knowing that every conversation with Al could be a little awkward. I politely asked if I could talk to him for a moment and I sat down on one of the couches that filled the upstairs of the Elk Lake boathouse. My most important question was whether I could or should move to the training centre in London, Ontario as my next step, regardless of whether I was carded. He told me that if I wanted to be the best, I absolutely needed to train with the best and see what the fastest women in Canada were up to. His opinion mirrored my intuition, but it was what he said next that finalized my decision to make the move. He told me that I would be welcomed. I am thankful to Al, as I needed to hear those words.

That fire that had been ignited the moment I sat in the Simon Fraser University novice eight in 2001 was the first chapter of my rowing career and now I was heading into the second chapter and the fire was stoked. The next step in the evolution of my athletic career: from university level rowing to national team rowing.

This tenacious spirit and belief in myself is a tool and character trait that I was fortunate to have sport reveal to me. In order to be successful I had to be willing to make moves without hesitation and shoot beyond what others might expect of me in order to achieve what I believed in my heart was possible.

Moving away from the comforts of home on the West Coast of Canada out to the unknowns of Ontario was not my ideal, but I knew it was what I had to do to make the team and the coach agreed. The decision was easy.

The Development Card

Sometimes I forget what I went through to get to the podium and that it wasn't all rainbows and sunshine. Perhaps it is easy to forget when you have had success at the end of the road because it makes all the struggles worthwhile. It is important to remember the journey as it was, however, because in recalling the memories I can gain much perspective. I realize now that the challenges and setbacks helped me get to where I wanted to go. It is the tests along the way that help remind me how badly I wanted something.

The struggles balanced with the successes along the way built my character, tenacity, and Olympian spirit. For me, the saying, "It is all about the journey," doesn't refer to the time we arrived in the Olympic village and until we competed. The journey includes the many years of training and racing that lead up to the Olympic Games.

For me, the path I was to follow in order to get where I wanted to go was clear in many ways. I would train with my university program and learn as much as I could for as long as I could and, when I had the opportunity, I was going to try out for the national team. The national team-training centre for women rowers being across the country over 4,000 kilometres away from home made travelling back and forth a solid commitment in time and finances, so I began with short stints out east when I could train with the group and get feedback from the coaches. I was open and willing to any opportunity I could get my hands on.

When I was finally officially training at the centre and brought into the fold, I became a part of the athlete pool that the coaches were choosing from and with that would come a "D" card. I wanted that card, but my path to a D card, like many athletes, was not cut and dried. I had been working tirelessly, but I wasn't quite showing the speed on "the erg" (what we called the indoor rowing machine *aka* an ergometer) that they were looking for. My status was put on hold with the condition that I would be given a D card if I were able to show improvement on my 6 km (kilometre) erg test. Two of our most basic erg tests were 2,000 m and 6,000 m, both gruelling in their own ways. That official acknowledgement of $500 per month became my training goal that moved me closer to my ultimate goal of competing at the world championships and then at the Olympics. It was definitely a nice fresh dangling carrot that I could use to fuel my training.

Having my funding put on hold gave me the sense that there was a hold on my progression toward becoming a Canadian Olympian. I could have looked at this as a sign that I didn't have it or that the coaches didn't think I had it in me and I do recall feeling disappointed that I wasn't an obvious choice, but I don't ever recall thinking that I didn't have the potential. It was that self-belief that fuelled me through the times when I wasn't getting acknowledgment from the outside world.

I wanted to row with the fastest women, to be one of the fastest women, and to wear that Canadian uniform; nothing was going to get in my way. Through this time in my development, I wasn't happy being on the cusp and working as hard as I was without getting acknowledged. This time was reminiscent of my earlier days on the bench in volleyball. My only choice was to find a way to keep my head down and keep working as hard as I could.

I was on a break visiting a friend in Montreal when I received notice via email officially stating that I was no longer on hold. This was a big step in the right direction. My hard work and dedication to my goal paid off and I felt validated. It was like Christmas morning to me. My national team journey had officially begun and I was ready to conquer my next goal of making a national team crew.

Perfection Is Unachievable

As a rower, I was always going after perfection, regardless of whether I knew well enough that it wasn't going to happen.

It is a real exercise for the obsessive-compulsive behaviour types. The idea of getting the perfect stroke, although actually unattainable, was how we spent our time regardless. We would just keep doing our absolute best with all of the cues and feedback we got along the way. Sometimes it would become exhausting, as I literally could never quite get it. Other times, likely when I had a bit more energy, I could go along stroke after stroke working for it without wavering.

Eight rowers moving toward that stern of the boat to catch the water in unison looks so beautiful and calm in appearance. Although it might seem that this is done in a calm and effortless fashion—and that would be the dream—it was rarely the case. There was a lot of information to juggle, whether it is following the body in front of me, conditions of the water, and our coach giving me feedback and telling me where to make changes in my stroke. It is like trying to rub your stomach and pat your head simultaneously. When a crew isn't moving together as one it can be very painful in the literal sense, as it could actually hurt our backs. On the other hand, it can take a hit to our egos if the boat is going painfully slowly and nothing we try would make it better.

This striving for great stroke after great stroke seemingly played into a deeper part of myself that doesn't think I am perfect at all. Rowing gave me a metaphorical bone to chew on and it was somewhat comforting and distracting from having to perfect other parts of myself. I wouldn't come to see the monster that I had created until I no longer had my rowing to critique.

What I now know that I perhaps haven't always known is that perfection does not lead to performance. We can strive for it, but we should always know that we have the ability to do extraordinary things without being perfect. It is our imperfections and our struggles that teach us the most. My shoulders were tight during my entire rowing career. I worked tirelessly on trying to loosen my shoulder muscles and engage my back muscles. Keeping my shoulders down and away from my ears was something I thought of on almost every stroke I took in the boat. I even came up with different ways to cue myself. I made improvements, but I was never perfect. It was working on my shortcomings that took me from being an okay rower to a great rower and a great contributor in the eight. Did I have to think about my shoulders still being tight on the day of my Olympic final? Yes, and despite this annoying imperfection, I still achieved a great result. Every one of us had something we were working on and I guarantee that every rower in the USA eight had something to work on too.

> It is our imperfections and our struggles that teach us the most.

Sometimes I think we look to people who have achieved big life goals and think that they must have something we don't have, but rather than having something we don't, they actually have something we also have. We all have internal battles, struggles, challenges, and areas we can improve. They are part of life and they can help to make us great.

> We all have internal battles, struggles, challenges, and areas we can improve. They are part of life and they can help to make us great.

A Life Motto from Sport: Find a Way

My coach, John Keogh, had a saying that I will never forget. I am sure each of my team members has her own moment or a saying that rings true to her, but for me it is John's "Find a way." He would say this to drive home his beliefs, to show that if we really wanted something we could always find a way to make it happen. It came up in many different contexts whether in a scenario where someone was whining about not being able to get a flight back to the centre in time for the first practice, or if someone was sitting on the rowing machine and the daunting little screen was giving them less-than-expected numerical feedback despite their best effort; he demanded they go harder.

This thought process changed my approach to sport and life. It has translated into my everyday routine. Obviously I have adapted it, but it ultimately comes down to being introspective enough to realize and recognize that if I truly want to make something happen, it is my choice to make the sacrifice or take the initiative to make it happen. Our current society doesn't often admit that the reason we don't do something or we fail at something is because we decided, perhaps subconsciously, that we simply didn't want it.

Not wanting something enough or at all is okay! Deciding to bail on something we start or moving on to something else should not be deemed as a failure; rather it can take a lot of bravery. I am better off putting my energy into the direction of my passions versus forcing myself to pursue something I don't care about. It is not only a waste of my time and energy, but of the time and energy of the people around me as well. The full quote reads, "Find a way, or find an excuse." I would say, don't bother with an excuse; just admit it's not what you want.

Acknowledging what it is that you want and don't want can

be addictively freeing. When I first came home, different social invitations I was not used to would arise and I often felt pangs of wanting to make excuses as to why I couldn't attend when I would rather stay in. Does anyone want to see you when you feel obligated to see him or her? I don't want to be the type of person who does things just for the sake of doing them. I would rather give a hundred percent and be present and feel good about what I am doing than feel resentful because I don't want to be there. If it is something we have to do and we have no choice in the matter, it is better to show up with a hundred percent and "find a way" to get through, than it would be to give up. If it's not necessary and it doesn't inspire you to action, be brave and change your trajectory. Find a way to do what makes you inspired, engaged, and happy.

> Find a way to do what makes you inspired, engaged, and happy.

Photo By: Marla Guloien

Chapter 6

Homecoming: From Hero to Zero

I had a realization early in my homecoming that humans unknowingly seem to be able to zone in on a delicate topic or question for someone else and then bring it up. It is actually quite comical if you pay attention to this happening; it is quite cringe-worthy actually. With me, it was "Oh cool, you won a silver. Who won the gold?" or "That is amazing. What are you going to do now?" I am sure everyone can relate or think of that sensitive question. If you have been in a relationship for a while it might be, "When are you popping the question?" or "When are you getting married?" If you just got married, it is always "When are you going to have a baby?" and if you just had a baby, it is "When is number two coming?"

Why, people? Why?

This is an interesting human behaviour, one that I have at moments wished we recognized as causing unnecessary torture. I have to remind myself that it is done with good intentions and is not meant to give me an anxiety attack or make me feel badly about my situation and myself; if it were, I could really lose my mind.

I have craftily recognized these topics and questions and prepared myself with my best and most confident responses. This makes me feel like I am putting on a bit of an act, but ultimately having the words ready makes it easier to cope with topics that don't make me feel the most confident. The other option would be to respond in a sarcastic and cheeky way, but my first suggestion is to maintain friendships.

When I returned home, my topmost sensitive question was definitely the one regarding my future. I decided the London 2012 Summer Olympics would be my last big race and I was ready to move ahead, but I didn't know how. I felt like the identity I'd had for so long was no longer mine and I wanted so badly to be able to have an answer to this question, specifically, to have an answer that felt as important and exciting as the journey and achievement that I was leaving behind. As an athlete, I loved making my country and my family proud and now I was and am addicted. How disappointing to have to tell people that I didn't have a clue what exciting endeavour I would take on next. I also struggled with feeling like I am not doing enough when I compare myself to my former Olympian self.

The combination of pressure I feel from the world wanting me to continue on a successful path and similar expectations I put on myself create an unbearable amount of weight to carry on my shoulders.

> Whether or not I have an Olympic medal hidden away in my underwear drawer, I am still just me, a human, not a super hero.

Recently, at an event, I was chatting with a very smart, sport-associated woman who said something that struck me. She said, "Athletes think that if they win a medal their life will change and then when it doesn't it is a letdown. On the other hand, the athletes who don't win medals think that their lives would have changed if they had and for them it is also a letdown." In a way, she is pointing out the losing battle of having so much riding on an end result and the change we expect from Olympic participation and success.

We have false expectations. Whether or not I have an Olympic medal hidden away in my underwear drawer, I am still just me, a human, not a super hero. Perhaps I additionally own the title of Olympian for the rest of my life, but I am still just me, Olympian me. I will still have to work for success and I am not phenomenal at everything. It is sad, but true, and no one wants to hear that, because it isn't glamorous.

This struggle—this confusion in purpose and status I have gone through and to some extent am still going through—is something you might wonder about; you might wonder if I saw it coming. Looking back at a quote I gave in London right after our final, it is obvious that I did see it coming. My response to the reporter of my local paper read, "'As of right now, this is it. There's nothing better,' the 32-year-old Guloien told *The Tri-City News* on her cell phone while heading to CTV's Olympic broadcast studio in London. 'I'm still going to work to try to achieve better in life in some way but right now, I'm not really sure how.'"

The question came hours after I'd crossed the finish line at Eton Dorney and you can hear in my answer that my wheels were already turning. I was already being prompted to answer what I didn't know and this question would only continue to grow into one of the most challenging and daunting questions of my post-athletic life.

What are you going to do now?

I was an all-in athlete who never came across something else that attracted me with even close to the same magnetism that rowing had. If I'd found that other calling organically then I would have been all over it, but I wasn't about to force myself to spend time on anything if it meant sacrificing training time or rest time.

> What are you going to do now?

Each athlete's journey is different and some will find the transition more challenging than others. I could have known what was next and had everything set up for me and would still have a hard time emotionally. Mentally preparing for the "what ifs" the way we did prior to heading to the Olympic games, as well as making a list of behavioural tools and resources can help to make the return leap into the real world easier. It is also okay to recognize the struggle, admit it is hard, and ask for help.

> It is also okay to recognize the struggle, admit it is hard, and ask for help.

A high performance athlete has been trained to exist and even thrive under pressure, but as these questions kept coming in my days after rowing, I didn't really feel like I was in thriving mode. When people asked me what I was going to do next, it felt as though they were pressuring me for an answer, but the pressure was actually coming from inside myself. For type-A sorts like me, pressure comes naturally. In reality, it isn't the person who asks the question who intends to press me, as they are simply being genuinely curious as to what I would be doing next. The pressure came from within and in transition from sport it hasn't really made me thrive when I didn't have the perspective of time, but rather it worked to hold me back and induce fear.

> My greatest strengths ironically can also be my greatest weaknesses.

To be able to self-critique and persevere under pressure is a sign of strength, but I realized during my days rowing that any strength can turn into a weakness. My greatest strengths ironically can also be my greatest weaknesses.

I laboured to perfect this balance of a patient, yet unbridled pursuit to perform throughout my athletic career. I saw many of my fellow rowers fail to maintain this balance and unfortunately it meant the end of their careers, mostly in scenarios where they pushed an injury when they should have been patient and given their body time. I feel like my strength was that I was and am a fearless go-getter who went after a dream, but I was self-aware and careful with my moves—I was wily at times and crafty enough to get what I wanted.

For instance, we would often do training rows in large packs of two-person crews (pairs rowing and doubles sculling) and single-person crews. These were occasions when I had to be crafty. I was neurotic about choosing my line and communicating with my partner so we never lost speed or got caught up in a cluster. I was borderline crazy about it at times. There was nothing more frustrating than getting caught up with another crew because I wasn't paying attention or not communicating. I was aggressive and I was tactical and for that reason I was not one to get left behind.

I was able to channel my energy positively with great success in rowing, but now that medium is gone and I have to channel my energy somewhere else. Coming off the Olympic high, I was running at high speed, ready for high performance. Even my Starbucks coffee could be served stronger! better! faster! When I was driving I felt like I was negotiating my moves like I would on the lake in a pack of boats. I was a crazy rower on the loose.

Once I was home and in some cases back on earth, I realized this pace was not something I could maintain without going crazy. I needed to shift back to a normal pace and reset myself in order to reintegrate into society. Recognizing these feelings, breathing consciously, and maintaining a physical routine and a healthy diet helped to keep my anxiety down and my patience up. When I let my physical routine of weekly (not necessarily daily) exercise go, ate poorly, and naively thought I could "go with the flow" and be flexible and relaxed in the way I saw other people behaving, I would get more overwhelmed with life than I ever had been.

> Coming off the Olympic high, I was running at high speed, ready for high performance. Even my Starbucks coffee could be served stronger! better! faster!

A top athlete can push beyond any benchmark of pain and is always willing to push a little bit more to be the best. We will also push ourselves on in times when a bit more patience is necessary. Being in transition and learning a new way of life are two of those times. Transition is a journey much like the journey of becoming an Olympian. It does not happen overnight and the platform and status of Olympic or athletic success do not simply transfer over to any and all future enterprises. It is humbling to go from being an expert in a field where I had achieved accolades and triumphs to being a newbie in every other arena, and hence from hero to zero.

This notion of zero is not one that we should shy away from. It is this feeling of starting over at rock bottom that we can use to redefine ourselves and get innovative with our future goals. "Who do you want to be next?" should be an exciting question to begin the process of transitioning. In letting go of who I was as a rower, I started to open up to the possibilities of who I might become in the future.

Photo By: Photobox Photography

Chapter 7

A Love Life outside Sport

If you are a full-time athlete—or a full-time anything for that matter—and you have managed to find someone to share a loving, lasting relationship with, then more power to you. On the other hand, you may be in my situation. I started rowing at twenty-one and I retired at thirty-three. The only seriously committed relationship I was really participating in was with rowing.

It wasn't until 2010 that I took the risk of opening my heart and added a love interest to my life. It felt risky to me at the time, but he ended up being a welcomed addition who provided me with balance outside rowing.

Mark was tremendously supportive of rowing; however, it

seemed our time together had a shelf life if I was to return to Vancouver after the Olympics. I lived and trained in London, Ontario but I was a hundred percent sure that Vancouver was to be my home. It was important for me to make this clear as I entered this relationship, but I think he secretly thought I would change my mind.

I did fall in love. I struggled every day, living in a different city and being away from my family. It was a testament to how much I loved rowing, but I knew it was for a finite amount of time and was a short-term commitment in the grand scheme of things, not a lifetime. The force that is my family is something that I could never compromise. I always looked ahead to the time when I would be back with my family when my rowing chapter ended. In the end, this was the deal breaker that led to Mark's and my relationship's demise. It was beyond hard to walk away from someone I pictured as being with forever.

Meeting someone caught me off guard as I had my head down, focused on training and training alone. I was sideswiped by fate and I followed my heart. I had never before felt as though I wanted to extend myself beyond the boathouse to anyone from the outside world.

He came along at the right time and it was refreshing to have something and someone outside my crew and my sport. I had a good system for myself as an athlete that had proven to be successful, but Mark gave me additional support that I never had as an athlete when I was in Ontario; he became my family outside my rowing family, which was all I had in Ontario before he came along. He was supportive of my crazy rower ways, and so we took our relationship to the next level and I moved in with him. Early on, it was a possibility that he might consider making the move to Vancouver with me one day, but months out from the games he decided that he would never leave Ontario. It was a hard pill for both of us to swallow, but we had to stay true to ourselves and we did just that.

It was the first time in my life that I was able to initiate walking away from a love interest, and this had become much more than an interest for me. In my younger days, I had always been the one who hung on way beyond the bitter end, even when the relationship was so obviously not right for me. I have used an analogy of a fallen water skier many times to illustrate this point. When a water skier falls they let go and wait for the boat to circle around and pick them up. In the sense of a relationship, I would do the opposite. I would be the fallen skier who would be too stubborn to let go. In my analogy, I could picture people in the boat yelling at me to let go the same way my friends and family had always advised me to let go of relationships once they were over and in most cases should be over. In this analogy, I could picture myself being too stubborn to let go, bouncing dramatically across the top of the water like a rag doll.

In this situation with Mark, I let go.

Olympic selection was looming and whether it was obvious or not, I had a sneaking suspicion that my time had come and it was going to be my turn on the chopping block. As much as I wanted, I couldn't stay in the relationship, let alone stay in that living arrangement, expecting him to support me through what was potentially going to be and became the biggest battle of my rowing career up until that point.

It wasn't as cut and dried as it might sound, as we all know that break-ups never really are. It took a few very tense conversations and many a tear leading up to making the decision to move out. Once the decision was made, there was no time for me to turn back. On my way to the boathouse, I stopped in at the house of my teammates, Rachelle Viinberg and Cristy Nurse, and asked if I could move in with them. Once they gave me the go-ahead, I booked a mover for the next day and went off to afternoon practice.

It was such a sad time, but it was also a bit of a blur. I had let myself picture my future with Mark and then I was packing it all away and diving deeper into my Olympic dream. I will never forget the move-out day. It was my first time living with someone and moving out was one of the hardest things I had ever done in any relationship. It was like a death for me, but I felt almost robotic or soldierlike in my mission to protect rowing.

I remember the first few weeks after moving out being really rough and then it was onwards and upwards. Perhaps it was rowing that was protecting me this time. After that initial stage, I cannot remember grieving or dwelling anymore. I was numbed as selection took over and took its hold on me. My pursuit of my Olympic seat turned out to be more intense than I could have imagined.

Fast forward to after our Olympic final when I no longer prioritized my rowing over my personal life. I was free to think outside the sport, free to analyze past and present relationships. Unintentionally, the end of my relationship all started to flood back into my heart and mind. While I was still in England, within a day of winning our medal, Mark reached out to congratulate our team on its success. It was great to hear from him and great hearing from someone back at home. It made me proud and excited because I had made him proud. He had been a huge part of my journey and my lead-up to the games. He had been there for many of my bright as well as my dark moments, and I am grateful for having had him in my life; I was happy to share our moment of glory with him.

Despite having been separated for almost a year, I was going

Chapter 7

through an aftershock of my break-up. I had told myself that I was going to party it up in London and have my final hoorah as an Olympian (the way people picture it—with condoms galore), but my heart was broken and I was now distracted and thinking about all that had happened.

Additionally, I was beginning another break-up; my relationship with rowing was now coming to an end.

Photo By: Photobox Photography

Chapter 8

Self-Belief over Doubt

My experiences have made me realize that no matter what anyone achieves or is pursuing, there will always be naysayers and doubters out there. Funnily enough, it is often the negative comments and people I cannot seem to forget and, annoyingly, I let them have the most impact on my mental state.

When someone calls out my idea or goal as being impossible, lofty, or unrealistic, it should never mean nor should I conclude that it is impossible. Doubting that something can be done is not an indication of whether or not it is possible, but simply an indication that doing it is not the norm.

When it came to my rowing plans, I was steadfast in my belief and direction. I cut out anyone who brought a "normal" way of thinking from the outside world if it meant my plans would be questioned. There were those who were either with me or against; fortunately, most of the people closest to me were on board, but I deleted a few Facebook friends along the way.

I will never forget when a friend—more of an acquaintance from high school days—asked me a seemingly harmless question about what I would do if I didn't make it to Beijing. At the time, I was home for the holidays from the London, Ontario training centre; the following season I would be facing selection for the Olympics. It was a valid question, but it reeked of disbelief in my dream, as well as misunderstanding the importance of the journey.

To go to the Olympics and win a medal is great, but it isn't enough to be the sole driving force for the kind of torture I endured over my rowing years. Very few people will achieve this goal in the end. Pursuing the Olympics has to be for the love of the sport and going after the dream, not whether you actually get there or not.

They say there is no such thing as a dumb question, but sometimes people ask questions that have layered meanings. I felt like she was probing for an explanation as to what I was really going to do with my life. I can say I let it go, but I never forgot the question and the way I let it make me feel.

Going to the Olympic Games and winning a medal for my country is dream-worthy material, and for most it stays that way. Of course, putting my life on the line and going for a chance to compete at the games was going to leave me successful or sent home. It seems cut and dried, and in many ways it is, but on the other hand, it is not that simple. It is a life experience that provides so much, regardless of the conclusion.

What I am most proud of and cherish are the journey, hard work, persistence, and sacrifice that it took to get an opportunity to be in the running. I would have felt lost and heartbroken if I hadn't made it, but I believed in what I was striving to accomplish enough that I didn't let myself think about the alternative—not often, at least. I knew that I was doing the right thing and quite frankly I knew the chips would fall where they may. It was my belief and ability to keep pushing for what I wanted without giving in to the possibility of failure that allowed me to come back from a last-place finish in Beijing to a silver-medal finish in London four years later.

Surrounding myself with people who live in a land of possibility helps me to see and achieve the greatness I am capable of. This is not some airy-fairy place where there is no realism. This is a place where dreams are achieved when you put in the work and have passion for the end goal. You must also have self-belief, because others will not always be on the same page as you and they will unintentionally (and sometimes intentionally) bring you down if you don't have your own healthy foundation of self-belief.

> Surrounding myself with people who live in a land of possibility helps me to see and achieve the greatness I am capable of.

My rowing career taught me what it feels like to have an unshakeable sense of purpose and drive to achieve an end goal. I have been less sure since I moved on from rowing, but I will never let anyone tell me that anything I want to do is impossible. I have experienced the close-to-impossible, and I am fortunate to have learned that the impossible can be possible.

Photo By: Dawna Guloien

Chapter 9

Struggling with Congratulations

Sometimes I have found myself struggling with the praise given for the achievement of winning an Olympic silver medal. To me, it feels a bit showy and self-righteous to take praise for my success. I hate to be a mood killer when someone is genuinely excited for me, so for the most part I do my best to embrace the praise and let the person be proud and excited for what I have accomplished. It is not that I am not proud or excited. Having spent much time reflecting on this discomfort, as well as analyzing why I might feel this way, I have come to some conclusions.

It is not about the medal itself.

I was part of a team. My success was not mine alone.

Competing at the Olympics is a privilege more than an opportunity to win a medal.

It was challenging for me as an individual, but the real task was to get in sync with others and be willing to sacrifice and compromise with between one and eight other people at any given time in any given crew. Personally, I was not meant to scull in a single for long periods of time. It was too lonely. For me, the single is nothing more than a vehicle to make it into a crew and to get faster to make a crew go faster.

Fame in amateur sport is not why I chose to become an athlete, but especially not a rower. There are no stars in the eight. We are training to blend into a single unit. We are trained to be egoless and selfless cogs in the bigger system of the crew. Rowing came first. It is a sacrifice, but when you want to be the best, it is an easy one. There was and is nothing more exhilarating than betting on yourself and laying it all on the line for something that you love.

These conclusions have ended up helping me to shift my mindset from feeling self-conscious when people congratulate me to accepting what a special journey I have been on.

It's Not about the Medal Itself

I don't like to be praised and acknowledged directly for the medal in and of itself. Although it gives my journey tangible credibility, it is not the most important part of what I did over the course of the thirteen years I was rowing. I loved to be able to make the home crowd proud and to make my family excited to share with friends that they knew someone competing at the Olympics. But in terms of everything I was proud of as an individual, all the achievement had already happened leading up to the games. The London Olympic Games were the finale and it was a big show, but without all that we had done to get there it would have been meaningless. What meant the most were the long, dark winters we as a team pushed through together; breaking my personal bests and my crewmates' bests on the rowing machine and the maximum weightlifting tests. It was managing rib stress fractures and pushing on when I felt like I had nothing more to give physically and mentally. It was the moments that only we saw that meant the most to me.

The winters were long. Without that focus of the summer months ahead and the competitions we were driving towards, they would have been unbearable. Being from the West Coast, I found the frigid temperatures of Ontario very uncomfortable. I felt like a wimp at times, but you tell me, since when do summer sport athletes break up the ice so they can get out on the water? We had some comical moments as we struggled and these made us tougher and stronger as a team and as individuals.

Mentally, winter was always a downtime in the year's training cycle also. The training group was large. There was always a sense that racing season was coming when the herd was starting to thin. A combination of survival and selection would solidify who would be the remaining athletes in contention for spots to represent our country. With the winter season, also came time off the water. During the months of December through to May, we would mostly be off the water unless we left Canada. Luckily, we travelled to three camps in Florida to break up our indoor training and get on the water. During our time at home in Ontario, there was a lot of physical testing and measuring of the team's strength and ability from a scientific perspective.

I would feel anxious wondering if I would still be fast when we got back on the water. It was hard to stay motivated through these downtimes, but the work we did was critical. You may have heard the quote, "Medals are won when no one is watching"; this says it all. Winter training is not glamorous, but it was when we made gains and built the foundation for successful summers filled with medals.

I Was Part of a Team

Everything we achieved was as a team and as a representation of our training group. I of course was a contributor, but to be congratulated as an individual feels strange when I competed as part of a team. Having walked away, I realize that what drove me was the group dynamic, my team, and the feeling that I was contributing to something bigger than myself. The harder I worked, the more I saw dividends in my sport.

The goals we strived for were the group's goals. The eight was a success because all the moving parts came together. I am most proud of what we did for this reason. We had chemistry, respect for one another, and we were truly stronger as a unit than we are as individuals. We were a small crew in stature, but we rowed with finesse, we rowed together, and we had heart. The bonds I built with my teammates will last a lifetime; so will the character and strength that sport revealed in me. I am proud of and grateful for the lessons I learned in how to go after what it is I want.

Competing at the Olympics Is a Privilege

Competing at the Olympics is a privilege more than it is an opportunity to win a medal. In the 2008 Beijing Summer Games when I was in the women's quad, we didn't have a medal-winning moment as we came in eighth out of the eight crews competing. Having experienced the polar opposite follow this result four years later, I know that my excitement and pride shone regardless of our placement. Coming together in peace to compete in a sport that we love is about so much more than the medals that are handed out at the end. It's about showcasing a country and a way of life, as well as exhibiting different sports and fields of play. What I love about the games are the athletes and their stories, the fierce competition, and the people surmounting adversities and giving it their all. These are what make me a lifelong fan of the Olympics.

> Coming together in peace to compete in a sport that we love is about so much more than the medals that are handed out at the end.

Don't get me wrong. It was definitely fun to come home and go to after-parties with some hardware to show off, because sharing the medal with people is my favourite part of having a medal. The front features a very traditional image of the Greek Goddess of Victory, Nike, and the back is filled with an abstract and modern design including the London Olympic logo. Each medal is also engraved along the bottom edge with the sport event at which the medal was won. I know from first-hand experience that it is less awkward to share that you have a silver medal than that you came last. Over and over again after owning my eighth-of-eight result, the conversation would shift toward something about being proud just to be at the games or how only a few ever compete on this world stage. It's true, but in that awkward moment, the conversation shift always felt like a consolation prize.

> My journey was about so much more than rowing. It was about relationships, personal development, overcoming adversity, and performing beyond my imagination.

My Olympic journeys gave me so much more than just a silver medal. As the years pass and I take time to reflect on all that I have learned and all of the relationships I have built over the years I rowed, I am constantly reminded and enlightened by the fact that my journey was about so much more than rowing. It was about relationships, personal development, overcoming adversity, and performing beyond my imagination, but to my capabilities.

Sport taught me so much about others and myself. In moments when I feel weak or someone says something that could potentially throw me into an insecure tailspin, I remember where I came from and what I am made of. I am passionate, aggressive, and I don't back down from a challenge. Sport also taught me to think ahead, react without hesitation, and do everything the best I can as efficiently as I can with persistence and dedication, even when things get hard. I can be afraid and I can admit it, but that is something that wouldn't hold me back when I was a rower, so it is not going to hold me back outside of rowing. Interestingly, the more vulnerable and honest about my struggle that I have been, the more I have found out that other people are vulnerable and scared as well. We are all just navigating through life trying to do our best with the tools we have.

> Sport taught me to think ahead, react without hesitation, and do everything the best I can as efficiently as I can with persistence and dedication, even when things get hard.

Sport also taught me to dare to be great and in doing so how to be more vulnerable than I had ever had to be formerly. As

I have mentioned, it was in the last few months leading up to the London Olympics and the naming of who would be in the team when I was the most vulnerable I had ever felt as an athlete. I had made the team for six years, every year since 2006, and I had always managed to position myself and rank myself in a place where I felt confident that I was going to represent the team and Canada.

> Sport taught me to dare to be great and in doing so how to be more vulnerable than I had ever had to be formerly.

Regardless of what I am proud of, I am more comfortable now with accepting the congratulations. The farther away from full-time training I get, the more I realize how physically phenomenal it all was. I was in the boat and doing it. I know that my body couldn't do that now. I am impressed with myself! Congratulations to me.

Photo By: Natalia Anja Photography

Chapter 10

Post-Traumatic Body Image

The two S's—success and stress—seem to go hand in hand. The last year of training was the most intense and testing time I faced in my career and, therefore, stressful. In an effort to get every last drop out of me, my coach was very demanding. Yes, he was demanding of us all, but I felt he seemed to pick me out of the crowd more often. It was completely nerve-racking.

There was one distinct instance when I recall hitting my limit. I felt critiqued by him to a threshold I was not willing to go beyond. I recall waving the white flag at him and telling him that whatever was happening was working more against me than for me. I could tell I'd started to be overcritical of my rowing as well as of our crew's rowing.

In my mind I could do nothing right: everything needed to be better and I was panicked it wouldn't happen in time. I felt like a fraud. How was I even good enough to be in my position if I was such a horrible rower? What I had done well to achieve my spot on the team had become an unknown in my mind.

My critiquing was not just associated with rowing either. It was much deeper than that. I started to critique my body as well. Body critiquing was not new terrain for me. I have always had a hard time with my body image, always feeling as though I wasn't thin enough or pretty enough. For the most part I have been able to overcome these insecurities through sport, as being strong became a priority over being supermodel thin.

Throughout my life, I have been affected by the messages I have received from the outside world regarding feminine beauty and even beauty standards for a female athlete. Once I was at a high level of rowing, a few daily practices were required that definitely brought up my insecurities and perceptions of how a female athlete should measure up. One trigger that heightened my insecurities was a ritual we had when we were travelling. Every morning we were to weigh ourselves in and have the hydration level of our urine taken. Early on in this process, we literally had a scale and a clipboard sitting outside the hotel dining room or in the lobby; this was quite horrifying to me. Depending on when I weighed in, I could see my teammates' data and no matter how hard I tried, I compared myself with others and determined my worth or rank from the numbers. The scale demons were haunting me. It was hard not to associate the scale with dieting, even if I was at a healthy body weight. Eventually, the coaching team realized this test could be done in a more sensitive way. From then on, we went to our strength coach's room and had these measurements taken more discretely.

Weight is a sensitive topic for most people. For an athlete, weight management is monitored in a clinical way to measure for any significant loss or gain that might negatively affect performance or health. I found it hard to separate the clinical view of my weight from the negative connotations I had developed about my weight over my life before sport.

At the London Games, my internal battle heightened when I didn't see my weight slowly drop toward competition as I expected. This was something I had seen in previous competitions and to me I felt like I was failing. I began weighing myself neurotically throughout the day. I knew it was wrong and I shouldn't have been spending my time that way, but I couldn't stop. I even felt self-conscious on the podium, wondering if my "gut" was showing and if I looked like the "fat" one. It was as though the weight demon had caught up to me and was beating me up.

I can look back now and see how outlandish it was for me to be feeling this way. It wasn't rational and I wish I could go back and refocus my energy correctly where it could have been better spent. Hindsight allows me to see what was going on and what was embroiling me in this turmoil.

Retirement was the next emotional hurdle and struggle that I anticipated was bound to bring up this body-image issue for me. I admittedly still struggle with these issues on a daily basis and always will. It is something that I managed to white knuckle through during most of my time rowing, but now as I work to rebuild myself and my life, I have had to recreate a balanced perception of what a healthy woman's body looks like and separate my self-worth from a number on a scale.

These days, I advocate for personal development and confidence building through sport, because being active and physically fit have been great ways for me to manage my body-image issues. I was lucky to find sport, because it is a really great outlet for anyone to train their body and mind for performance, rather than for looks. During times when I felt insecure, I depended on the structure of the training environment and the support of my teammates who always made me feel that I was an asset they believed in. The skills I developed in sport taught me and continue to teach me to do so much more than just how to be a great athlete. I have also learned how to perform under adverse conditions, be they internal or external or both.

Outside sport, the typical woman on television and in magazines does not look the way I look, and that has been enough to cause me to struggle internally with my looks. Most women, like me, are far less glamorous, slim, and groomed than the versions of women we see on television. I am smart enough and self-aware enough that I know this thought process and pressure of keeping up to this image is irrational. I know I have beauty inside and out, and I am thankful that I have my health. It is also important to me that I stand strong for little girls and women who see me as a role model of strength. I do not want to disappoint them with these seemingly trivial battles. I am an Olympian, for crying out loud!

I would hope that we all have better things to focus on and so much more to be thankful for. This is a much bigger conversation. Although I wish I could overcome my negative body image with all that I am thankful for, it is not that easy. At the end of the day, I am human and I have the same worries and insecurities as everyone else. It hasn't been easy to change my mind about my body insecurities, so it has to be a choice and a practice. Just like anything else, the more we practise, the easier it will be. I would rather be honest and be myself and be someone young women can look to because I am human and I struggle just like many people out there, rather than be someone who pretends they don't deal with insecurities on a daily basis.

It is important for my mental and physical health to keep working out and eating well as a lifestyle beyond being a full-time training athlete. Detraining from full-time sport training to training for lifestyle is necessary to maintain balance. Essentially, detraining programs are weaning processes from a full-time regimen to a more real-life amount of physical training to create balance in life. Coming from being a "soldier" in a team sport, I was so burnt out and exhausted that the last thing I wanted to do was ask for a program to follow. In hindsight, I should have asked for a program and followed it.

It took me two years to recognize and embrace that I cannot stay in Olympian shape for the rest of my life. That fitness level wouldn't be as special as it was if it were something I could maintain forever with any level of ease. Sadly, in some ways, it was only meant to last for a brief capsule of time.

Retirement and the succeeding transition is a process. It will be different for each person, but for everyone it will happen and no matter how much pressure I put on myself I could not force it to happen the way I thought it should.

This journey can be almost metaphorical and poetic at times, as it applies to so many other lessons and experiences in life.

Chapter 11

Saying Goodbye to My Sport

Retirement or Divorce from Sport?

I refer to leaving my career as a professional rower as "retirement," but the more I talk with other people about it, the more I think I could refer to it as a "divorce." It's not like I finished a career in the sense that most people do when they retire. When people think of retirement, they think of freedom, moving on from the shackles of work life, and slowing down to do the things they haven't been able to do while they were working. Mmm. That's not exactly what I feel I am going through. Perhaps it is true that after rowing there is freedom from the shackles of a strict training regime that allowed for little else, but I am just beginning a new career. This is why I think of it as a divorce, divorce in the sense that it is the termination and dissolving of a bond or a tie in my life.

I haven't experienced divorce in the marital sense myself, but there is still plenty of time for that. All kidding aside, I have talked to many people who have and I understand that they feel a sense of loss, stress, and a sense that they are starting over again. It can be exciting and scary all at the same time and that is what I am feeling!

When I tell people that I have retired from rowing, a subset of people responds with, "That must be nice." They associate retirement from sport to retirement at age sixty-five. Now would those same people relate better to what I am really experiencing if I said I just got divorced from sport?

It is as though I met "the one" in 2001. In 2006, my relationship became official when I made my first national team crew after spending five years working really hard on our relationship. Although rowing and I had big goals for the future, a key difference is that we did not promise forever to each other in the same sense that real couples do. Arguably, however, that is not true. I gave a large piece of myself and my heart to rowing and rowing will be a part of me forever regardless of whether we are together. There were ups and downs, but ultimately "we" wanted to go for the long haul. After the 2008 Olympics in Beijing, we felt we had grown apart and amicably we parted ways, or so we thought. I thought we had achieved that ultimate goal when I had competed at an Olympic Games and I packed up and moved home thinking that I was ready for a divorce/ retirement. What I soon realized was that there was more to be done and after a brief separation we were back on to go to London and bring home a medal for Canada.

Ultimately, both divorce and retirement have their challenges.

Transition is hard no matter how happy you are about the change or how necessary it might be.

Grieving Sport

The loss I felt when I retired from rowing was gut-wrenching. Did I accomplish all I was meant to accomplish? Was the accomplishment the pinnacle?

To understand the loss we feel as athletes when we transition from full-time sport to our lives afterwards, it might be beneficial to go back and understand why exactly sport, in my case rowing, was so important and significant. More than the medal, more than the Olympics, the training lifestyle became the sole focus of my life, from the moment in 2001 when I first sat in a boat and was challenged with keeping it upright to my last World Cup in Sydney, Australia in March 2013. It wasn't just about the rowing itself; it was always about something bigger than that.

> When I try to explain my motivation for the sport, I answer the same thing because the answer has never changed. It was always about the people.

When I try to explain my motivation for the sport, I answer the same thing because the answer has never changed. It was always about the people. Rowing took me outside myself.

In 2010, I was competing in the Rowing World Cup I with my teammate Ashley Brzozowicz in the women's pair. She also got married that month. Trying to choose when to get married is not only a monumental decision because it is a huge life event, but trying to choose a time that didn't interfere with a rowing obligation was close to impossible. World cup season two years out from the Olympic Games was a solid bet; however, it was still a total juggling act for Ashley. I honestly don't know how she did it. Her wedding was the Saturday before a 2,000 m ergometer test on the following Monday, which was going to be trying for me, and I was just a guest at the wedding. I can't imagine how it would be for a bride.

The evening of Ashley's wedding, I looked down at my feet to see that they were completely swollen. I ran out the door to hail a cab. As anyone who has ever pulled a 2 km test on an ergometer, or even rowed on an ergometer, can attest, my body was going to hurt really badly regardless; but doing too much that Saturday would make it far worse. It's not like I could just wing it either; performance is expected and the pressure is always on.

Ashley is and was a class act through this time as well. She embraced her situation and showed up like a champ. She hid any stress and exhaustion she felt from us because she didn't want to burden us with her life outside rowing. That is something that a great teammate would do out of respect and consideration for her team, but we are human and I could definitely empathize with how hard that must have been.

The following weekend, Ashley and I left town for Bled, Slovenia. A beautiful European getaway for her honeymoon—but she was with me instead of her husband, Roy, who was back in Ontario! She never whined or complained about the sacrifice she made, not even once. Most likely, it was not her ideal honeymoon, but we made the most of it ... we won the first world cup of the season in the women's pair! It was the first sign of progress coming out of our camp after a downturn in performance and coaching. This was a really exciting time for Canada's women's program. It was a once-in-an-athletic-career-seizing-the-moment time. We were elated with the progress we were making on the rowing team. It was well worth all the sacrifices she had made that month.

Losing that foundation of strength and friendship that I had with my crew was a huge loss when I retired. It was my rowing bubble where I had grown to feel safe. Timelines and goals were set for me and as long as I kept marching and held my head up, I felt as though I was moving forward. Deep down, despite the tough moments, I was always driven by my passion for my sport, as well as my belief that I could achieve something really special with the group of athletes I was with. It was a gift to be given in life. I believe I was meant to find that in rowing: to serve a life purpose that I felt I was absolutely meant to do.

When I really dug into my emotions, I never came to the conclusion that my life was over or complete. There was, however, a very strong feeling of loss and grief. And I feared and doubted where I was to focus my energy next. This unknown world of possibility that should have been exciting and in certain moments was exciting, also sometimes felt more like a nightmare as I was transitioning, endeavouring to figure out what was next.

Spending time with the people I love, meeting new people, and trying new things have helped me get through this time and fill the void that leaving rowing created. Coming from a team sport, I was used to training with up to twenty women, three times per day. Group exercise classes at community studios are great places for me to be around a large group of people for workouts. They make me feel like I am at home. I am a team player, so I rarely work out by myself. Finding that deeper drive and purpose is also essential. As I have mentioned, helping others and contributing to a larger cause is a driving passion of mine. I found that passion in my rowing journey and I have found it since in advocating for sport, storytelling, speaking about my journey, and leading spin classes.

If I'm Not a Rower, Who Am I?

Who will I be to people if not Krista, the athlete, the rower, the Olympian? Although, I am also a daughter, sister, granddaughter, niece, cousin, friend, and teammate—to name a few identities—I have spent a great portion of my life dedicated to sport. Being so intently focused on one goal, Olympic gold in rowing, makes me feel most connected to the identity of "athlete." I have other interests, like cycling, travelling, and fashion. But rowing took top position in my life for so many years that it is hard for me to think of myself separate from my experiences as a rower. As a challenge, I have imagined leaving it out when I introduce myself to new people. Imagining this is as far as I have got, as I have never been able to come up with an honest way to explain how I have used my time over the last ten plus years. It might not be all of who I am, but it sure feels like it was all that I was doing.

This label or box that we as athletes become so attached to can start to make us feel like we are nothing else. I went from having a title that carried prestige, to not knowing what label to use for myself. Announcing I was an athlete training for the Olympics was sexy and exciting and it was fun to make people feel proud and excited about my work. What am I now? Am I a washed-up, recovering Olympian? A divorced rower? Am I in between jobs? That sounds so cliché.

There is a silver lining that should be recognized. Beyond sport, the exciting part is that I can shape my identity. Moving on meant shedding the outer layer of my rower identity and presenting myself to the world as another version of Krista.

My identity shapes my actions. As an athlete, I acted like an athlete and made life choices based on what an athlete would do. When I was no longer the athlete I had been, I felt like I had lost my sense of direction. Beyond rowing, who would I be to the outside world? This was a question I couldn't answer; therefore, what was I to do with myself? It is a question every athlete needs to face and to some extent I am still facing it.

In new encounters, people often share their professions. It is a great way to understand a person, as we learn how others spend most of their time, but it was a hard question for me to answer. Do we have to answer this question? Do we need to place ourselves in boxes? Who is this system of identification for? We are all so many things. I recommend we take the pressure off our shoulders when it comes to defining ourselves by stating what we do. Who do you choose to *be*? Now that is a question that allows for some flexibility, forward thinking, and creativity.

I decided I was an author and an entrepreneur before publishing my book and starting a business. Those are labels and identifiers that mean something to me and drive me to choose my actions accordingly. What would an author do? What would an entrepreneur do? We should become what it is we want to be before we have the title. Acting the part or faking it till you make it gets us making choices and taking steps as if we are already there and that is ultimately what will shape our pathway to that end result. An author writes. Can you publish a book without doing the work of writing that book? You are an author if you are writing and producing written content for a book. Let's not get caught up on the end result, but focus on the journey. As athletes, we can become fixated on our results to a point that is detrimental. It is not about what I have accomplished that makes me who I am. It is about the journey. I am more than my achievements.

> I am more than my achievements.

Chapter 12

Adjusting to Post-Olympic Life

Slowing Down. What Is the Hurry?

If I could go back and have a chat with my younger self, I would tell her not to be so hard on herself. The standards by which I measure myself are unrealistic. Training to become an Olympian fuelled the beast in many ways. When I was training, the term "on time" was specific and strict. For us, being on time meant being five to ten minutes (sometimes even more) early and ready to go with a hundred percent focus. Nothing less was accepted without ridicule. I am a conscientious person, so this was a rule I followed diligently. Over time, I learned to appreciate it and adopted it as a motto of my own. It kept everyone on point. It is much more efficient if you are not waiting around for people in order to get something done.

I appreciate a good sense of order and the training environment provided me with this. Structure, rules, and consistent patterns definitely play into my routine-dependent personality. In the real world, however, this sense of order creates an unrealistic expectation. There are other factors and life priorities that change the dynamics. If you gave everyone a lashing for being late you would be very busy giving lashings.

It was a culture shock to re-enter the real world when I first moved home to Vancouver. Back in the city after living in a suburb of London, Ontario as an Olympic athlete, I found that no one was ever on time. Not the way I know "on time" to be. I found myself sitting and waiting a lot. On the odd times I would find myself stuck in traffic and late, I felt extremely anxious.

My sister, Marla, and I have had countless squabbles over being on time. She can relax and let timeframes adapt, whereas if I set a time I cannot let it go. If I say 5:30 p.m., I mean 5:25 p.m. and definitely not 5:45 p.m. If we are going out together, she hates it when I stare at her in the last fifteen minutes when I am ready to go and she is still getting ready. Leave it to sisters to really push each other's limits. I think she would even agree that I have relaxed a bit over time. I picked up on the trend and relaxed into it. I say this as if I had much choice, but I suppose there is always a choice. It is rare for me to be late to this day, but I don't stress as much. Old habits die hard, as they say.

For twelve years, I trained with consistent routines, goals, and timelines. I thrived in this environment. Following schedules and a regimen comfort me, even if I whine and complain when I feel limited by their confines. I like to know where and when I am expected. Additionally, I work well if I know what is expected of me. Once I retired, it was not as easy to manufacture a schedule because the motivation to keep it up isn't there. Not there like it was, at least.

Chapter 12

One Priority or Many

Other adjustments for me were the realization and
understanding that in the real world everyone has different
priorities from my own. In rowing, we all had one priority, or
least a well-defined top priority—gold. Everything we did all
day every day was for an Olympic medal. Anything else we
chose to have in our lives outside rowing was second to rowing.
Leading up to the games, anyone close to us would vouch that
it was all about the medal, different from in the real world
where people balance priorities, sometimes multiple priorities.

When I was working at Lululemon, I worked alongside or
with others who had different "top" priorities and things going
on in their lives. One person might feel ready to go for the
next promotion, while a colleague might be keeping her hours
in check while she tries for a baby or plans a wedding. This is
expected and respected in the real world.

In striving for the Olympics, there are only the Olympics.
I grew to feel most accomplished working with others in the
Olympic environment.

What Can Top the Olympics?

What do I want as much as I wanted to represent Canada
at the Olympics and bring home a medal? It is an unrealistic
question, with a whole list of associated assumptions and
expectations, but nonetheless, it crept into my mind recently.

There is nothing that can replace the intensity and spirit of
the Olympics. That is what makes it so special. It is the intensity
that I miss the most: that passion and drive for an end goal; a
mental and physical state that is impossible to maintain. As an
athlete, I still yearn for that intense feeling.

Some components of this past time of my life may certainly come along for the next chapter, but it is also important to be open and excited about all that will change. In reconnecting with myself, I have explored questions like "What motivates me?" and "What inspires me? What gets me up in the morning?"

Photo By: Photobox Photography

Chapter 13
You Are Enough

"Good enough" is never enough in sport. Complacency is like death. This mentality keeps you driven, keeps you hungry, and keeps you performing. At the same time, it is important to remember that you as a person are enough.

It is important to separate the person from what he or she does. I find this hard to do at times. I have measured my worth based on my performance. Looking back at my journey with the perspective I have today, I can see that I am so much more than the athlete who participated in two Olympic Games.

If I had gone to two Olympics, then the next athlete had gone to three. If I won one medal, then the next athlete won two, or even six! Records are being constantly set and broken. Hardcore-ness is obtained and then some other crazy specimen of sport comes along and shatters expectations and sets the bar even higher. Very few records and accomplishments sit unchallenged for long.

It is humbling to know that there is always someone achieving more. This can also breed a culture and a way of thinking that believes nothing is ever worthy of being sufficient. Mostly I realise that my achievements in sport were more than sufficient, but when I am being hard on myself, I don't think that way. I can tell by things other athletes have said to me that they don't feel that way about themselves either. I hear things like, "Well, my sport career wasn't as big as yours" or "I never got to the level you did." Regardless of our achievements, sport teaches us all similar lessons that we can speak to universally. Let's think of ourselves as athletes as we would think of our own child. If it were my child who brought home a silver medal and did what I did, I would be endlessly proud. Why am I not as gentle and proud of myself as I would be with my child (who doesn't even exist yet)?

> If it were my child who brought home a silver medal and did what I did, I would be endlessly proud. Why am I not as gentle and proud of myself as I would be with my child (who doesn't even exist yet)?

When your internal voice starts to gang up on you, turn it around. Ask yourself how you would talk to a younger version of yourself. Would you tell her she is beautiful and deserves unconditional love and support despite her flaws, or would you belittle her and break her down for every little nit-picky thing you can find? The answer seems obvious when I think about it, but it's not as easy when my internal critic is in charge.

For instance, do you think you are beautiful? That is a hard question for me to answer. I have never thought of myself as beautiful. I have moments when I feel self-confident that I am attractive, but I have other times when I feel hideous. A bad image at a horrible angle can quickly turn into evidence that I am utterly unsightly. Why do I focus on what is outside myself to answer this question? We live in a visual world filled with access to all sorts of images. Current day cameras and photographic software used to enhance images unfortunately alter what we see and can make us feel less than adequate in comparisons to others. What I have learned through my experiences is that things are not as they appear. From the outside, my life looks a certain way. I have great photos on my Instagram and a list of achievements that are impressive, but I don't feel inside what you might expect if you reviewed my Instagram account. I have struggled with self-esteem since I was a young girl; the struggle was most intense in my school years. Retiring from rowing brought back much insecurity to the forefront of my daily life.

There was never a time I can recall when I felt more empowered and confident than I did when I was rowing. It became a great arena in which I could push myself and build confidence. I found strength in belonging to a group of like-minded women. We were like-minded, as well as being alike in body type and skill set. Outside the rowing world, I am always one of the tallest women around, which has always made me feel mammoth. Instead of appreciating what has become a gift, I loathed it. In rowing, I was one of many tall women and sometimes even the shortest.

Being five foot ten made me short, relatively speaking, in a pool of athletes. I remember standing tall, even wanting to be taller! This was such an astonishing shift in mindset and it came simply from being around others like me. I no longer felt as though I stood out; I didn't feel insecure about my height: I owned it.

The camaraderie and understanding I received from my teammates gave me strength. The safe place I found in the world of rowing allowed me to explore who I am and who I want to be. Being empowered and confident, I began to see what I was truly capable of.

Leaving rowing and re-entering a world where I am once again the tallest female, sometimes the tallest person in the room, brings back many a demon for me. Now I have the armour of a silver medal and a purpose for which I used this height, but it doesn't mean that my feelings of wanting to hide away from standing out have disappeared.

Chapter 14

Life after Rowing

I have been extremely impatient with where I am in life after rowing. I retired aged thirty-three and created new life goals: start a career, find a soul mate (not just a husband), build a family of my own, and reconnect with friends and family. It would be challenging to do this on the best of days, but even more challenging after falling into a mini depression.

It wasn't long before I was in a deep depression and I went to the doctor and was prescribed an anti-anxiety prescription. I didn't feel like I was going to snap out of it on my own without help. I also saw a counsellor who helped me to release some of the anxiety and worry I was feeling about the status of my progress or what I perceived as my lack of progress beyond the games.

Getting out to meet new people is really the last thing I wanted to do. Luckily, I have great friends and family members who have been sympathetic and patient with me and always gently (sometimes, not so gently) remind me that I need to get out. Working through these feelings has not been a quick process; I worked through this for a solid year. Along the way, there were peaks and valleys when I felt like I was moving forward before falling back. I never took the anti-anxiety medication with any consistency. Once I acknowledged that I was struggling with depression and started talking to people about it, I started to feel better.

Despite feeling like I was getting a bit more traction with my mood stability, I was still not quite heading in the direction I wanted to go. "Where do I want to go?" was still the question haunting me and without knowing this, how could I move forward?

After I completed a one-year fashion-merchandising program at Blanche Macdonald Centre, I got a job working at one of Vancouver's Lululemon Athletica athletic-wear stores. A few months later I was transferred to work at the head office on the ecommerce team. On paper that might sound like progress, but I wasn't happy or satisfied. By summer 2015, two years into my retirement, I was still not in a relationship and I had quit my job at Lululemon's head office to make my next move forward.

I have continually reminded myself that this transition is a process, much like the one I was in over the twelve years I spent on Canada's national rowing team. Nothing came easily and nothing came quickly. There was one significant difference and that was that rowing had deadlines and we focused on the ultimate end goal. I ask myself, "What is the point of everything I am doing now that I am no longer rowing? What do I want out of life? What makes me happy?"

I always knew what I was competing for and what I was training for in rowing; but in life beyond I sometimes don't see my next move coming because there is far more choice; I couldn't come up with the answers and this made me feel lost. These lost moments when I felt like I had no direction made me feel extremely low.

When it comes to trying to know what I want to do with my life in terms of a career, I often get asked what it is that I like to do and what makes me happy. That has been an interesting question, which at times I have not been sure how to answer. I didn't even like rowing that much at the end, as I put myself under so much physical and emotional stress that I started to resent it. I know that today if I sat in a boat and pulled an oar through the water, my heart would probably beat with excitement and love for the sport that gave me so much and that I truly enjoyed.

Other than rowing and outside of rowing, "What is it that makes me tick?" is the question of the day.

When I talk to other people about my transition from sport and open up regarding some of the pain points in my journey, I frequently get responses from others who are feeling the same way. I have felt alone at times, but it really doesn't take long before someone shares his or her struggle, bringing me right back into the universe. People all experience transition, whether it's leaving a job to start a new one, taking a job out of school, or divorcing after having been married for seventeen years and starting anew. We are all trying to find our way in the big world; transition is the human condition.

There is so much more diversity in life outside the athletic world. At times, the outside world can be a very confusing place. I put myself out into the universe as much as I can on a daily basis (some days more than on others) and I know that one day, my life is going to come together in a very fulfilling way. It already is coming together.

> Transition is the human condition.

Helping others by sharing the story of my journey has become my new purpose and end goal. I am doing that through my writing and through speaking to people about the lessons I have learned along the way.

There are so many ways that I can help people. Now that I know that helping people makes me happy, I can work towards actions that will serve that goal. It is conversations with people that help me to reflect on my current situation and the thoughts and questions I have about life. I am constantly and pleasantly surprised by how much we can learn from each other if we open up and share our authentic selves. Through this sharing I have learned that I don't have to share the strong athlete self whom I worked so hard to train and develop. My true, vulnerable, and authentic self is much more effective at communicating and I learn and give a lot more when I share that part of myself with others.

It is important for me to be a role model for others who is

relatable and real, whether I am giving a keynote speech, or leading a workshop with a corporate group discussing teamwork and the road to success, or having a more informal conversation with young girls about setting goals and dreaming big. My stance is and will always be that I am not special or better than anyone else and I accomplished something extraordinary in spite of this. This to me means that anyone can. I want to empower anyone to channel his or her own inner Olympian in or out of sport.

> My stance is and will always be that I am not special or better than anyone else and I accomplished something extraordinary in spite of this. This to me means that anyone can.

Photo By: Kevin Light

Chapter 15

My Mom, My Strength, My Perspective

My mom has had degenerative scoliosis since she was thirteen years old. She has lived with its symptoms—pain, stiffness, nerve pain, and muscle spasms—most of her life, but as she has aged, the condition has really taken its toll on her body. Shortly after I came home and was no longer rowing, she had major spine surgery to fuse her spine in place. The hope was that this drastic measure would give her body some stability, limit any further detrimental progression of her spinal curvature and, most importantly, stop her pain.

Watching someone I love live in a constant state of pain is very hard. I can only imagine and empathize how hard it is for her. She is one of the strongest people I know. She is the matriarch and the glue in our family. Her pain can only be seen by those closest to her, as she is never without a smile and she never slows down.

The surgery and post-surgery recovery were like nothing I have ever seen anyone go through in my entire life. On May 6, 2014, she went in for the first of two surgeries; her surgeons went in through her lower abdomen and fused her lowest vertebrae, as well as cleaned up any degeneration they could find. Then, after spending just over twenty-four hours recovering from what was a major surgery on its own, she went in for her second surgery on May 8, 2014. This second surgery required the top spinal team in our country to drill screws into each individual vertebra, followed by screwing them into a metal rod that would sit along her spine acting as a stabilizer. It took over twelve hours of surgery, in which she was face down being pumped full of fluids while being opened up from her upper back to her tailbone and having metal rods and screws added to her insides.

I have a pretty solid stomach, but I was unprepared to go into the postoperative care unit the morning after Mom's surgery. Knowing our family member would be so drugged that she wouldn't even remember seeing us in this state couldn't stop my dad, sisters, and me from visiting her to make sure she knew we were rooting for her. My dad and I went in to see her together; she was only allowed two visitors at a time. Leah and Marla waited to go in on the second wave. I had to take a nurse's chair when I saw Mom. Not only was she unrecognizably puffy from the massive amounts of fluid in her system, she also started to try and tell my dad and me something and she couldn't get out more than a furrowed brow and some strained grumbles. My heart rate probably spiked to where it was in the last 500 metres of my Olympics race. All I wanted was to give her what she needed, but it was anyone's guess. We even gave her a clipboard to try and write on, but that was useless as well. My dad was so gentle with her and seeing his worry gave me a whole other level of stress. But he stayed composed and rubbed her forehead to calm her. After she had calmed to some extent, we went out to pass the torch to Leah and Marla. I warned them, but there is no stopping this family from being by each other's sides. My dad and I waited for them to come out; they were just as shell-shocked as we were.

As a family, we had no idea what we were going to endure over the next few weeks. Mom was completely incoherent and in a state of dementia, which can be caused from the anaesthetic in a long surgery. It was probably best for her and worst for us. In my life and in our family, my mom is always the person I go to and talk to when any sort of chaos occurs. At this time, I really felt I needed to talk to her.

Despite the stress we were under, taking care of someone while they are foggy can have its comical moments. At one time she thought she was at a Canucks game waving to her very own 550,000 (the digit she came up with) followers—she was waving a peace sign to all of her fans who were up in the ceiling. She was very complimentary of my style and wardrobe as well. I appreciated that, of course.

It was not so funny when one of her doctors told my sister that sometimes anaesthetic can trigger an early onset of dementia that would be permanent. He expressed how worried he was that she was not more alert; he said there was a possibility she would not come out of her confused state. Complete meltdown. That was seriously not an option I could even fathom. By the grace of some higher power, the fog started to lift within twenty-four hours and my mom started to come back to us.

Coming out of the mental fog was a cakewalk relative to the physical work she had to do over the course of her recovery.

She would have to learn how to walk again before she would be allowed to go home. Still in a bit of a mental fog, she was determined and focused to check off the list of things she had to accomplish in order to go home. My sisters and I don't have to look far to find where we get our drive and competitive spirit. She was walking down the hall within two weeks of her surgery. Nothing can hold this woman down.

A year and a half later, she is still dealing with far too much pain on a daily basis. Unfortunately, the rod did not stand up to the pressure of her body and broke. She has now had additional surgery and it looks as though she will have even more surgery down the road. After going through this ordeal, I know she hoped for better results, we all did. I am not sure that she would ever willingly go back to do it all again. We will never really know how things would have turned out if we had taken a different fork in the road, but I believe she did the right thing. I hope that one day she lives a pain-free existence.

I aspire to have the personal strength and resilience I see in her. She is an unstoppable force in so many ways. My mom has always been the person I look to for advice in life. She has never steered me wrong and she has always believed in me, letting me know I am capable of anything I put my mind to. The human spirit she displays daily in order to overcome such physical adversity is phenomenal.

She has been through a lot in her life: a few of her hurdles include undergoing three pregnancies and C-sections, raising three children, losing her brother and her father when she was in her early thirties, all while managing constant pain. All the hardships and pain she suffers and continues to endure in life make me realize how tough and resilient we all can be.

I know for myself that seeing my mom after her operation reminded me of what is really important in life, and why I feel content with being back home close to my family. I am fortunate to have been so healthy during my rowing career, but I am also grateful that my family stayed healthy as well. Only two things could have ended my pursuit: not being selected to the team and my family needing me. The second was one of my "what if" questions. I had worked through what I would do if something were to happen to one of my family members and I knew I would have left without batting an eyelash. I would have had more regret missing out on being with my family and helping them than I would have regretted not going to the games. I feel lucky that I never had to come to that crossroad and make that decision.

Chapter 16

My First Half Marathon

In order to explore my newfound freedom and to maintain my fitness and health, I started eating a Paleo diet of lean protein, vegetables, and healthy fats; I joined CrossFit; and I signed up for a half marathon as well as for the GranFondo 120 km cycling event from Vancouver to Whistler. Not exactly a light training load, but these seemed like the right things to do to keep up the momentum. I just couldn't fathom taking a break and relaxing. I was motivated by the fear that if I took a break, I would lose my fitness and gain weight. The only way I knew how to maintain my current state was to do what I had been doing.

I was my own worst enemy and I didn't set myself up for success, in taking on so much during this time. In the end, I didn't train consistently and, for fear of hurting myself or embarrassing myself, I didn't complete either the run or the ride. I also quit CrossFit and the Paleo diet. The events stayed on my goal sheet, but it wasn't until the second time I registered for the half marathon and GranFondo that I managed to complete them both. It literally took registering, not completing, feeling guilty, registering again, and doing some preparation (not a lot) to get me out there for these events. It came down to integrity. I said I was going to do something and I wasn't about to fail myself again. I might be a bit stubborn.

> I didn't know how to do athletic events for fun either.

I wasn't ready when I registered the first time, but I didn't know that. I didn't know how to do athletic events for fun either. Not shockingly, my motivation and consistency with my training was not what it was for the Olympics. I will never be that prepared or that conditioned for an event and I can now accept that. I know now that it might be painful (on the ego and the body), but it can still be fun. A key goal-setting tip that my experiences exemplified is that if you want to feel like you are succeeding and achieving your goals, it is best to set modest and attainable fitness goals and outperform.

Chapter 16

> It is best to set modest and attainable fitness goals and outperform.

My biggest fitness-related accomplishment after rowing became the half marathon. Running has always daunted me and if you ask any of my rowing teammates, they would tell you that I was not inclined to run often, if ever. I had it in my mind that I shouldn't run in order to protect myself from potential injury and excessive knee pain, which I experienced when I ran. I couldn't fathom having an activity stop me from being able to row, especially when it wasn't one that I particularly enjoyed.

Once I had retired from rowing, my perspective changed. Running is such an accessible activity and there are tons of fun events and locations to explore on foot. Completing a half marathon was something that I decided I wanted to have under my belt, so for the second time, I signed up for the SeaWheeze Lululemon Half Marathon on August 15, 2015. I was prepared to make it happen the second time around.

I managed to exercise my procrastination muscle during the lead-up to the event. I could have and should have joined a running group, knowing that I am driven by being in a group environment; I'm not as consistent and dedicated when it comes to being an individual athlete. The team environment takes the calibre of my work and my ability to achieve up several notches. It has been a challenge for me to develop the skill set of working on my own, to create intrinsic motivators in an effort to improve this factor, and to allow myself to not only excel in a group environment, but also in a lone state.

I did run a few times throughout the year and managed to cling to a fairly high level of fitness through spinning indoors and cycling outdoors, albeit not at an Olympic level. One week out from my first half marathon, I was not feeling prepared. I hadn't run more than ten kilometres in one go in my life! It was a bit disappointing and odd for me to have set myself up so poorly for something that I declared I wanted to do. I guess I never declared that I wanted to do it well. Perhaps the fear of not being able to excel at or even finish a half marathon was holding me back. Perhaps the stakes were not high enough and I didn't see how I was doing it for anyone else but myself. The reasons for not training more remain a bit of a mystery.

Urgency snapped me out of my procrastinated state on the Monday before the Saturday half marathon. I set out to run fifteen kilometres and see if my body would even let me do this event. It is one thing to push through pain, but I have experienced having my knee literally stop bending while running and there was no way that I was going to injure myself when I had now put myself in a position of being so ill-prepared. Fuelled by curiosity and panic that the countdown was on, I was able to run fifteen kilometres without dying and only experienced minor knee pain near the end. I broke down a mental barrier on that day. Now I knew that the distance would be totally achievable. What's another six kilometres? Ha-ha.

I spent the rest of the week essentially hobbling around in soreness. I still wasn't walking freely on the Friday, which gave me only twenty-four hours left to recover. But that was all I needed. I set my mind to it then and there was no turning back.

Once I was fully engaged, albeit rather late in the game, I utilized all the tricks that sport had taught me as I was seeing them come to life through my event-day preparations. I had been sore many times before and I knew how to work through it. The morning of the 7 a.m. race, I woke up at 4:45 a.m. and did a light spin on the stationary bike and stretched in my apartment gym to wake up and get the blood flowing. This was something that I pulled out of my tickle trunk of rowing tricks, as it was a common practice we used in our racing. It is important to make sure to be up three to six hours before any event so that the race is not the first time the body gets moving. I then got myself ready and rubbed tiger balm all over my knees, which was also a rowing trick. I loved that stuff when I was training. The tingly feeling and even the smell made me think of healing muscles.

I had a partner in crime on that morning as well. My youngest sister Marla had decided she would join me on this crazy adventure; she had trained even less. Marla actually really likes running and is always up for an adventure, so she stepped in and entered. Leading up to the weekend, we had some funny moments googling potential running injuries. We were not exactly on a textbook training plan. Regardless of the information we found on the internet, we managed to turn our increasingly worried minds around a few days out and we actually got pumped for being in the race. That morning when I came back to my apartment she was also preparing, but in a different way. She had a bath, blow-dried her hair, and did her makeup! She is a singer, songwriter, fashion designer, and entrepreneur, and she was set to get cute selfies! It was quite the morning.

The biggest nugget from this experience was I learned that this is what real life events should be about. If I had trained, this day would have had a more businesslike approach and my expectations would have been much higher. My lack of preparation forced me to relax, lower my expectations, and have fun with it. My sister and I pumped each other up, laughed, took selfies, and bonded as we descended upon the Vancouver Convention Centre in a cab surrounded by droves of brightly coloured Lulu-clad individuals. We nervously laughed and peed numerous times before we stood among the tons of people ready to set out on a 21.1 km excursion. Lining up for the porta-potty reminded me of what a nervous bladder feels like.

> My lack of preparation forced me to relax, lower my expectations, and have fun with it.

Management of the nervous pee had been built into my pre-race warm up when I was rowing. No detail was left unturned. When my bladder would get tense, I found that I would have to go again right after peeing. My pre-race ritual, therefore, included five minutes when I could have my final pee approximately fifteen to twenty minutes before we would leave for our on-the-water warm-up. Keep in mind the tricky balance in rowing, because once we launch there could be fifty to sixty minutes before we would be racing. If I didn't want to perch precariously over the edge of the boat then I would either have to hold it or start the race feeling like my bladder was about to burst. My teammates teased me that I had a small bladder when I was over the edge of the boat precariously or while I peed into a sock so that it would be absorbed and not splash around in the boat. Not exactly glamorous, but a solid memory of the lengths we went to.

It is such character-building moments that I don't always remember until they are jarred by new experiences, like this run.

I ended up completing my first half marathon in just over two hours and I was extremely proud of myself and thankful for a body that allowed me to accomplish a goal such as this. I hadn't set myself up in a way that had made it easy; however, with my residual fitness and mental vigour gained from years of rowing, I was able to pull it off.

I don't always realize it, but after spending years in a sport striving for greatness on a world stage there is an Olympian mindset that has become part of who I am and it is a common thread in all that I do. Whether it is being physically aware and in tune with my body, programmed to think about hydration, or being able to juggle the thoughts of pain, boredom, and fatigue that entered my mind while setting out on a two-or-more-hour workout.

The Olympic spirit is one of persistence, resilience, mental fortitude, determination, and adaptability. I was reminded of these traits throughout my run as I saw glimmering moments come to fruition. I was able to spend most of my time running reflecting on these things and really appreciating all that I had gone through and learned to get me to this point. Whether in my warm-up strategy, or in the last two kilometres as I broke down the distance in my head in the way I had in my rowing races. It is because of rowing that I am able to see my full potential in the moments when I was driven to do absolutely whatever it took to be the best I could be, not only for myself, but also for my teammates and my country.

> The Olympic spirit is one of persistence, resilience, mental fortitude, determination, and adaptability.

This half-marathon experience reminded me again of my favourite quote, "Sports do not build character. They reveal it."

Photo By: Photobox Photography

Chapter 17

Leaving One Opportunity to Find Another

Figuring out what I don't want to do with my life is as important as finding what I do want. I have struggled with this. At times I have felt afraid because I sometimes feel like I don't want to do anything.

In June 2015 after being at Lululemon for nine months, I made the decision to venture out and leave behind the role I had established. Although some might think my position would have been a great fit, I found myself struggling to make it work. Interestingly, when I gave my notice, the manager who had brought me on initially was not shocked. She told me that she had thought I would not be there long, but she thought

I would be there longer than nine months. I like to think of this as a testament to myself and my ability to recognize when something doesn't fit my path, and so did she.

Through my time at Lulu, I realized and learned many things about myself. One is that I can be impatient in relationships, work, and sport. I will work relentlessly for something when I decide it is what I want. This drive and the motivation are great, but I have sometimes got myself into a bit of a pickle when I assume things will take less time than they do; that's when I become impatient. Impatience with a side of relentless self-critiquing is a wicked combo. To say that this can be derailing is an understatement.

> Impatience with a side of relentless self-critiquing is a wicked combo.

When I first started in my role on Lululemon's ecommerce team, I wanted to be able to support the team and contribute right away. I felt insecure and horrible for not being up to speed, but I had no right to be up to speed. I needed to take a breath and give myself a break. I was my own worst enemy.

As an athlete, I used my fixation on performance to my advantage in the sense that it drove me. I was trained to go for that edge and take on more. Now, outside sport, I have to tone down this fixation. Lack of patience can lead to impulsive decision-making and that is where mistakes can be costly. Fixating on performance and being impatient don't go together so well. For example, in relationships I have scared people away because I am "too intense." I want too much too soon and I am unable to go with the flow. That being said, anyone who knows—let alone has dated—an athlete would probably agree that athletes are intense individuals. They have to be intense in order to do the things that athletes do.

Self-reflection has led me to scrutinize how my rowing experiences shaped my intense, cutthroat, and impatient mentality. The stakes in Olympic rowing are do or die. I didn't go with the flow in a four-year quadrennial cycle. It is now or never; you are either in or you are out. Indisputably, real life seems to have more scenarios in which flexibility is welcomed.

I am in a different place in life than most people at my age. Up to their mid-thirties, most people have been shaping their career, their relationship, and their family. I am trying to do it all now, simultaneously. The difference isn't what makes it hard though. It is the immense amount of pressure I put on myself.

> I am not willing to settle. I don't want okay, enough, or mediocre.

I am realizing that the more I push for where I think I should be, the more isolated, alone, and annoyed I become. This doesn't make anything better. I was going through the peak of this mental turmoil during my time at Lulu, and inevitably it drove me to walk away from a role I didn't want and a lifestyle that wasn't working for me. In my decision to stand for something else, I felt a sense of peace and comfort. I literally said the words to my manager and a weight fell off my shoulders. Everyone was very supportive of my decision.

I am not willing to settle. I don't want okay, enough, or mediocre. I was a great rower, I was part of a great crew, and I loved the way that felt. I am not willing to settle and neither should you. So as I often say, you either go big or you go home. I am going to continue to work tirelessly and relentlessly to find whatever it is that ignites my passion. I will, however, also try a small side of patience with the ferocity I have. I don't want to send people running for the hills.

Although it was hard to walk away from the small amount of stability I managed to create for myself in finding a full-time job, I needed to walk away to give myself the space to find out what it is I *want* to do. I have thought of it like being in a relationship that doesn't make you a hundred percent happy. I was hard pressed to find happiness when I was putting my time and energy in the wrong place. Chances are it wasn't going to happen if I didn't make a change. I am not willing to take those chances.

Photo By: Mike Murray

Chapter 18

Training the Mind to Be Present

I hear people talking about "being present" often. This notion of being present in the moment has become more challenging in today's world with all the stimuli we have coming at us at all times.

In the world of sport, distraction can mean missing the

podium or never reaching one's potential. That focus visible in the eyes of the athletes on television is pure presence and it has been trained and practised, as well as tested over time.

> That focus visible in the eyes of the athletes on television is pure presence and it has been trained and practised, as well as tested over time.

How do I apply this phenomenon to life outside a boat? What is my end goal in life? To be happy? To be loved? To have a successful career? To build something I'm proud of? Perhaps for you, like me, it is all of the above. It is a tall order to fill and not concrete in its direction. What would that look like?

What is your end goal? What makes you happy? Perhaps you know and you are in pursuit of the goals that fulfill you.

For me, finding my next thing to focus on has been a work in progress. After I achieved the goal of winning a medal, I lost that drive and the feeling that I was pursuing something big. It has taken some time, but I now find happiness in not only pursuing my goals, but also in helping others to become empowered to live their dreams. For example, writing, speaking, and sharing my perspective with others are ways in which I am setting out to achieve my big-picture goal of serving others. It makes me happy to help people and that is by definition a pursuit bigger than myself. That is the legacy I want to leave behind. Now that I have this direction, it is important for me to set goals and to stay present and focused in pursuit of my life's calling, not in a tunnel-vision kind of way, but in a clear-minded approach that allows me to contribute to the bigger picture and have the direction I had when I was rowing.

If we agree that in order to accomplish what we dream to

achieve it is important to stay in the moment, focus on the journey, and avoid fixating on the end result, how does one do this?

The answer could be simple, but the practice is not. It is complex and it is built over time. Honing in on each mission en route to achieving whatever is down the road is how you train your ability to zone in to the present. It really is an exercise in patience and task management. The benchmarks reached along the way help create a sense of slowing down and taking the time; achieving these steps helps with the impatience we sometimes feel when we have a big goal to achieve. Quotes like "Rome was not built in a day" speak to the notion of patience and success built over time.

Our rowing team set goals for each session, each day, each month, and each year leading up to the Olympic finale of the quadrennial. We were constantly working as a team to accomplish benchmarks we had set ourselves. We also kept track of these stepping stones, either through journaling, adding to a memory board on our training centre wall, or simply reminding each other in words of encouragement within a workout when we needed a little pick-me-up. Sometimes, our encouraging words were more grunts and cries versus actual words; but we knew what they meant. Every time we walked into the training centre en route to the changing room to suit up for another workout, we passed a wall of achievements and memories. While resting between sets we could glance over and be reminded of where we had been and why we were doing what we were doing.

It is as important to remember where you have been as much as it is to think about where you want to go. In a culture where we are endlessly critical of ourselves, we sometimes forget how great we are and what steps we have taken and the accomplishments that got us to where we are today. I challenge you to find a way of documenting your journey and keeping note of what it took to get to where you are today. In doing so you are producing personal words of inspiration to remind yourself that you have exactly what you need as the foundation for your success.

> In a culture where we are endlessly critical of ourselves, we sometimes forget how great we are and what steps we have taken and the accomplishments that got us to where we are today.

I have had to take this step-by-step mentality with myself in my transition from sport life to post-sport life. It is not always easy. In my darkest moments, I find myself struggling and frustrated that I am not where I want to be. I'm impatient! There have been lonely moments during my transition from sport when I have felt like an outsider; as though the only place I belonged was in the rowing community. I didn't know what I had to offer. Without identifying as a rower, I felt like I am not doing anything with my life and I have no skill set. These times and feelings felt heavy and insurmountable.

When you are not strong enough in the moment to come up with the reminder you need to surge ahead, it is helpful to create a network of people who will remind you. When I was competing, that network was my team. We could talk about anything and, in sharing my deepest frustrations, I would always feel understood and inspired to push through whatever it was I needed to do to get to the next benchmark. If not my teammates, my mom, dad, and sisters have been and always will be my foundation.

Surround yourself with people who make you feel understood

and can remind you of how far you have come. Your own words journaled in past moments when you felt accomplished and strong could also be a place to receive strength. Ultimately, you don't have to be alone in your struggle. For every dark thought and doubt we have as humans; someone out there is feeling the same way or has felt the same way at some point. I have also noticed that every self-doubt I fixate on has a positive and uplifting counterpart that I am usually missing. It is as simple as a change in perspective to get to that more positive place and frame of mind.

> I have also noticed that every self-doubt I fixate on has a positive and uplifting counterpart that I am usually missing.

I remember one day when I was feeling as though I didn't know where I belonged or what I should be doing with my life. I was unhappy that I was feeling this way at thirty-five years old, since my younger self's vision of thirty-five was quite different. I shared this with a friend. I told her that I felt I should be farther ahead than I was; she listened. She then went on to share with me that she felt the same way. Despite our different circumstances, she has had the same dark moments and struggles, and a light bulb went off for me. Part of me felt badly for whining, but another part of me felt grateful to hear her rebuttal. I realized all our individual struggles are relative to our circumstances. In a strange way she offered me a sense of belonging and a jolt of inspiration to acknowledge that everyone has their challenges and to push on just like everyone else.

The path to success doesn't change regardless of what your

end goals are or what you have achieved in the past. We all need to have benchmarks along the way. Breaking down any goal into smaller, measurable pieces allows you to be present and focused on the moment versus looking too far down the road. A current goal of mine is to deliver a sixty-minute keynote speech in which I will convey key takeaways from my rowing journey and transition beyond the finish line. In order to get there, I have started by taking on speaking appearances where I just share a five-to-ten-minute vignette from my story. In doing so, I am also getting used to speaking in front of a crowd and sharing my story about who I am. I have also worked with a speaking coach who has helped me to communicate better and to present myself confidently in front of a crowd. I feel as though I have a story to tell, but I am right there with the majority of the population when I say that public speaking is scary! Facing my fears and getting strong enough to overcome barriers and limiting factors are extremely satisfying benchmarks. Like anything else, it gets easier the more I do it. Not easy, but easier.

> Breaking down any goal into smaller, measurable pieces allows you to be present and focused on the moment versus looking too far down the road.

These steps help to keep me in the moment and focused on the process versus being overwhelmed with the daunting goal of standing in front of a large crowd and delivering a sixty-minute memorized speech. My life team—including coaches, peers, family, and friends—also helps keep me going when I slip back and start to feel doubtful or discouraged. I have had to be reminded that the process I took when I was rowing is no different from the process I am taking now. The circumstances have changed, but the road to success is no different.

Photo By: Mike Murray

Chapter 19

Glass Half Empty or Glass Half Full?

My good friend Sara likes to send me random questions to get my wheels turning. It has become extra fun in our friendship. As she was on an analyzing spree one day, observing people, she was curious about my thought on the topic of the glass half full versus the glass half empty. Secretly anticipating my answer, she asked me how I saw the glass.

My answer was that I am a glass-half-full person when it comes to the bigger picture. I believe that life is good and I am thankful for all that I have. When it comes to "going after it," I can see that the glass might not be full, so, therefore, half empty. If it were possible to fill it, then why wouldn't we try?

Is it possible to fill the half-empty glass? If you believe it is possible, going after the full glass would most definitely require going outside the box and your comfort zone. Most people are okay to stay in their comfort zone and are happy to have their glass the way it is; they might not go after anything more. I believe it comes down to a personal choice, but I also think that this is a game of perception. Each person's glass and each person's comfort zone is on a sliding scale. Sara's full glass is not necessarily my full glass, despite the fact that we are both goal-setting high achievers.

Going after my full glass and pursuing the Olympic dream were not outside my comfort zone, though all that came with them pushed my boundaries. Moving away from home plus the exhausting hours of training and rowing in sub-zero temperatures put me outside the zone. But the actual pursuit and the unorthodox life choice were within the zone. Perhaps I should not go as far as to say I was comfortable there, but it was inviting. I accepted the abnormality of it.

Now transitioning to find my new identity has tested the limits of my comfort zone. I have set the bar for what can be obtained by achieving Olympic success. I am in some ways my own motivation to go after what is abnormal to achieve great things. Writing a book, teaching spin, and public speaking in an effort to help others through my experiences are my new pursuits. Am I comfortable? Heck, no! I want to be pushing the zone's parameters and, therefore, I must be doing something right.

> Writing a book, teaching spin, and public speaking in an effort to help others through my experiences are my new pursuits.

It is my belief that it is outside our comfort zones where the real action happens. This is where we can truly test ourselves and see what we are capable of; we can even surprise ourselves with our capabilities. We shouldn't shy away from pushing our limitations. Since leaving high-performance rowing, I have taken on different projects, all of which have brought me to where I am now. I am fuelled by the enthusiasm for success and curiosity for what might be.

Regardless of where I have been in any single moment along the way, one thing has always remained. I believe that I am capable of achieving great things and making the world a better place. The process and the journey build up our character and make us into the people we imagine ourselves to be.

Appreciate what you have and never be afraid to go for the full glass.

> Appreciate what you have and never be afraid to go for the full glass.

Photo By: Marla Guloien

Chapter 20

Fitness and Pressure

Fitness and sport are big parts of my life and always will be. Making sure that I keep working out has been a helpful way to stay feeling sane through my career shift. I really notice a change in how I feel and how I react to my environment when I don't work out consistently. That is the thing with "real life" in comparison to the life of an Olympian. In real life, we sometimes have things that are bigger priorities than working out and we have to adapt.

When I was training, I was able to push myself to absolute exhaustion for multiple hours a day, six days per week, because I could then spend every other waking moment fuelling and resting for my next session. In a balanced life, you have to do your workout and then function in all of your other responsibilities. That becomes a skill in itself. I feel very lucky that in my Olympic training years, I was able to focus my energy toward becoming the best athlete I could be. It was a selfish pursuit at times, but it was a necessary evil.

Spin classes, otherwise known as indoor cycling classes, have always been one of my top choices when it comes to indoor activities. This type of group fitness class was the foundation of my fitness training before my days as a rower even began. It has been great to get back into it and there is no shortage of spin studios in Vancouver.

I have a Spinning Instructor Certification, but I also did apprenticeship style training at my favourite studio to prepare to lead my own classes. The format was very laid back, with little to no pressure or tight timelines on my performance. Any pressure I felt, I put on myself. If you have been taking in anything I have said, you will now know that I put a fair share of pressure on myself.

The habit of pressuring myself follows me wherever I go, with whatever I do. It is literally hard for me to clean my apartment, train my dogs, or order a coffee without doing it in a high-performance manner. I am constantly self-critiquing and it can be quite exhausting. Where does this come from? One might wonder if this is related to sport and my training. I personally feel I came by it honestly; however, I have trained my habits. It is a great strength to be self-aware and critical of your performance, to a point. As I have mentioned previously, all strengths can also be weaknesses if imbalanced.

During my training to lead spin classes of my own, I received an assignment to prepare five songs so I could go through a shortened version of a typical eleven-song session with my trainer. I invited my sisters to come along and be supportive subjects. I was as nervous that morning as though I was going in for an official audition where the stakes were much higher than in reality. Was this Olympic selection? I was a bit confused by my nervousness. As I admitted this to my sisters that morning, I started to tear up. I laughed at myself because I was fearful of telling them what to do in this new environment. Ask my sisters or any of my teammates if they ever felt I was afraid to tell them what to do and I am sure you would get a resounding, sassy "No." I can't imagine one of them saying that I wasn't a little on the bossy (I like to think "assertive") side when I want something done. Where was this nervousness coming from?

Marla is a stellar cheerleader and she simply reminded me, "You got this girl; you are an Olympian!"

She was right! I am so much stronger than I was feeling. This is why you need family and a support network. I was definitely working through strong feelings of vulnerability and I needed a cheerleader.

My five songs went over well, although there is always room for improvement. As I was reminded, no one was going to live or die over a spin class. My trainer gave me the reins to relax and bring it down a notch, but my internal voice wasn't letting me off the hook that easily. At the end, I received some helpful and constructive feedback. My trainer, manager, and friend, Natasha, let me know that I seemed surprisingly shy in the beginning as I warmed up to teaching. She was surprised because she did not see me as a shy person. I told her I am shy and she quite confidently let me know that I am not, ha-ha. I must hide it well.

I have been vulnerable and fearful during my time branching into a new arena. I belonged and was established for so long as a rower, a national team athlete, and an Olympian. Now, there is the sense that I am back to square one and I have to learn new things. Starting over has made me feel weak. It is hard for me to let go of being the expert and at the end of the day, I want success and to be the best. Aside from wanting to achieve, I have realized that I am also trying to avoid failure, but that can't be done. Fear of failure was not only gripping me: it was holding me back. Failure is not something that can be avoided and we can't learn something without making mistakes. The only way to avoid failure would be to avoid progress and I decided I can't do that, so I have to embrace it.

> The only way to avoid failure would be to avoid progress and I decided I can't do that, so I have to embrace it.

I also realized that I am not always one hundred percent aware about how I show up to others. It is interesting that someone like me can show up as strong, confident, and outgoing when I feel weak, insecure, and shy. I feel weak and shy much more often than I would like to admit. Luckily for me, I think the majority of people see me as strong, confident, and outgoing. This way I can fake it until I make it!

When I am on, I am on. When I feel passionate about something, I am at my best. The shy, insecure version of myself is usually well-hidden, but she comes out at the most inconvenient times! For example, during a first date, or when I stand in front of a room to speak, or at a networking event, and even when I am teaching a spin audition. I mockingly refer to this extension of my personality as "she." *She* really isn't a welcome addition, but she comes on strong and is rather unpredictable. I suppose my sassy outgoing side can be equally so, but that isn't as bad because that side of myself makes me proud and is entertaining. *She*, on the other hand, makes me feel weak and unworthy of success and quite frankly *she* is not invited out anymore. My new strategy, having had my spin experience the other day, is to recognize when I am feeling this way and tell myself to shelve it. I am going to tell myself that this side of me is not helping and is not invited to participate in any way that inhibits my ability to move forward.

Not being an expert at anything outside of rowing and instead feeling a sense of loss when it comes to my past expertise have made me feel like I have lost control of my life. Where do I belong now? I feel a sense of panic in terms of finding something and finding it fast.

I have felt so left behind, regardless of this feeling having validity. Knowing I am notoriously hard on myself, I have had to remind myself that I am not the only one going through this. There are many people who feel this way and didn't have an athletic career or win an Olympic medal. It seems that everyone I talk to feels or has felt this way at some point or another. We live in a day and age where it is more and more common to change careers more than once in our lifetimes. Something we need at these times is patience. We need to take time through our transitions to find new paths. To anyone approaching this point in his or her transition, I would say you must embrace that you are going to feel a sense of loss no matter how hard you fight it. I will say it over and over. Be as proactive as you can to prepare for this time, let yourself be vulnerable, communicate, reach out for help, be strong, believe in your ability to endure, and most importantly, be patient!

> To anyone approaching this point in his or her transition, I would say you must embrace that you are going to feel a sense of loss no matter how hard you fight it.

There are days when I literally and figuratively have to be pulled out of bed and into the world. In this interim phase of rebuilding myself, rebranding myself, and pursuing an entrepreneurial career, there are days when I feel like maybe I have taken the wrong path. I, like many people out there, suffer from the overachiever syndrome. I am writing a book (this book), learning how to coach indoor cycling classes, as well as learning to and being coached on how to build and express a high-level keynote speech. I wake up feeling like it isn't enough, I am not talented enough, and I am essentially not enough.

This internal struggle with belief and self-doubt has been something that I have fought my whole life. It is my struggle and yours may be different, but nonetheless I am sure you have something you struggle with. I anticipate that I will always be dealing with and struggling with self-doubts. I have come to terms with this fact and embraced that it makes me normal. It is why I am writing this book. People don't like to talk aloud about where and how they struggle. Really successful people especially. Perhaps this is because they have branded themselves on their success. Vulnerability is not always sexy.

> Vulnerability is not always sexy.

Stories of overcoming adversity are plentiful in our society but, after that adversity is overcome, is everything perfect? I think we assume that success comes with freedom from our demons, but they come along with us wherever we go. The lessons we learn when we are successful, despite our weaknesses, adversity, and challenges, are the ones that should carry noteworthy significance.

I believed passionately in rowing. My abilities to make a boat go fast were proven. There isn't any moment in time that outclasses the instances when I hunkered down while rowing and pushed for every second and every inch. I remember workouts where I would get into a tunnel of focus that felt superhuman. I would arrive at the top of the rowing stroke ready to drive my oar through the water harder than I had ever accelerated before and I would throw my body into it with reckless abandon as if it were the last and only stroke I would have to take … and then I would do it again and again and again.

There was a time when I lost touch with my strengths as a rower, teammate, and athlete and I asked my coach, John, what he saw as my key strength. He responded by telling me that he could see when I was fired up. He knew I was in an unstoppable place from the way I rowed in those moments. The people around you are the best mirrors of your strengths. They can remind us of why we should be confident.

Attaining a seat in an Olympic crew was hard, but we were also fighting to take our boat from a world-class silver-medal-winning boat to a gold-medal-winning boat. Every inch we could get the boat ahead would count. Every second, half second, quarter of a second faster were moves in the right direction. It is shocking how dynamic it feels to go one second faster over five hundred metres. That is the thing with rowing. From the outside it looks like a string of bodies moving harmoniously in sync with seemingly little to no effort, but inside it is lively and animated. In every stroke and every moment we are reacting to stay in sync, whether the water changes, a gust of wind hits the starboard side, someone has a weird stroke, or someone was going through her technical focuses. Additional work was also prompted from the outside by the coxswain, the coach, or a teammate.

The idea of feeling pain and struggle while not showing it on the outside is something sport teaches us. I remember there being a call out in the boat to ensure we all had a relaxed face. You don't want to be using your energy scrunching your face or letting anyone know you are close to your limit. These are referred to as physical "tells" in cycling. Opponents watch for body language to show weakness before they attack, essentially kicking their opponents while they are down; we as athletes know that it is harder to counterattack when we are weak. Competitive sport is about staying focused and going as hard as you can physically muster, all the while showing no pain on the outside.

> Competitive sport is about staying focused and going as hard as you can physically muster, all the while showing no pain on the outside.

Photo By: Mike Murray

Chapter 21

A Career after Rowing

Looking for a Job

I have had moments when I wanted to get a job, any job! Not a dream job, not a job I would be happy doing, but just a job to fill my time. I did some research online and found out that job searching online is daunting. The only roles that I would be qualified for are entry-level positions. As much as I might want a job, I also want to feel engaged and motivated to do what I do. I am not opposed to being in an entry-level position per se, but I feel like I am capable of more.

It is somewhat shocking to me that I am not worth more in the job market. Whether this is reality or not, this is how it makes me feel. I am sure many others feel the same. Years of training as an athlete, whether representing my country and winning medals or not, do not transfer directly to the resume.

Feeling like I have no skill set after a twelve-year commitment to my sport made me feel like a complete outsider. My goal is to have a successful career doing what I love. I know the hard knocks speech that at the end of the day I just have to bring home a paycheque, while doing the work regardless of liking it, but I refuse to give in and give up. I will not give up on what I know deep down is attainable and no one else should either. I am referring to you!

In my time rowing, I was spoon-fed almost every move regarding my career. The progression of achievements was pretty much laid out for me. It was a shock to my system to be suddenly responsible for my next move. At first, I felt a sense of freedom. I could do all the things that I hadn't been able to do and see all the people that I had neglected, especially in the last two years of my career. But it didn't take long for the excitement to fade and I was feeling more grief and uneasiness than freedom and excitement. Just when I started to feel as though I didn't know what I should do with myself, the feelings of pressure to be successful with the next project started to build.

It was easy to get caught up in the fact that I didn't have a laid-out plan for my future, but in order to figure out what it is that I want to do I had to brainstorm. In these days of the internet, there are many websites that can at the very least get your juices flowing and help get you out of a funk. Here is an example of one that I used: www.theguardian.com/lifeandstyle/2014/nov/11/-sp-questionnaire-what-job-would-make-you-happiest. It sets out a selection of questions that help you to see where your interests lie and how those interests point you towards certain career choices, for instance, enjoying working with customers ... or not. I found that the questions helped me get my creative juices flowing and directed my thinking toward career choices.

Motivation: Showing Up for Others

Knowing what I always wanted to do as a child helped me come to some clarity about this question. I always wanted to be a police officer. It wasn't just so I would have a gun and people would, therefore, listen to me, even though I have joked about that. It was the desire to help and protect people.

I have always been extremely motivated to protect. I think this stems from having a very protective mother and two younger sisters. I have always taken on that role of the protector in our family. When I come to the aid of another person, I get a rush. It is a special rush, similar to the rush and drive that rowing gave me. It is tireless and energetic. Much time can go by and I won't notice if I am helping someone else. That to me is a measure of passion for something. What stops time for you?

> What stops time for you?

What is the driving force that kept me doing what I did day in and day out for the thirteen years I was rowing? I was motivated to show up for my crewmates. I fell in love with rowing as part of a team. There was nothing like being that close to the water and gliding along it early in the morning as the sun came up. It wasn't long before the season changed and it was cold, rainy, and miserable and I lay in bed dreading that 4:50 a.m. alarm. If I didn't know that there would be a handful of women showing up at 5:30 a.m. to set out on the water to get stronger, better, and faster, I would have hit that snooze button a hundred times over. My teammates were a built-in motivator for me and that gave me the incentive and drive I needed to make sure I showed up. I loved rowing, but I love sleep more. When it was fun, it was more fun as a team. When it wasn't fun, I was glad I was not alone. We suffered as a team. Through the extreme heat, humidity, rain, snow, sleet, ice, burning legs, and shredded hands, we did it together.

> I am inspired to show up for others. This is something that I need to incorporate into my post-rowing life. "How can I make a living out of this motivation?"

I felt like I couldn't breathe, and my mind was screaming random incomplete sentences—I wish I could have recorded my inner monologue during racing—combinations of technical cues, swear words, and incomplete sets of counting from one to ten. My body responded knowingly to the pain I had trained it to embrace and amazingly it kept functioning. Despite information that my legs might be sending to my brain, my body and mind became separate. We would not stop for anything but the line. That was a commitment to each other.

I am not saying that rowing is a selfless endeavour. The key was that I was contributing. Whether that was as a team member in a crew or anywhere in life. I realize that when I feel I am needed, I am driven to show up and give my all. The real challenge is that I was confident, passionate, and fulfilled by what I was doing for the past twelve years and now I am lost trying to find what I will do next. In this transition phase, I am struggling to find that same passion for something else.

I am inspired to show up for others. This is something that

I need to incorporate into my post-rowing life. "How can I make a living out of this motivation?" is my next question. Policing, nursing, coaching, speaking—I have considered them all, and sharing my story to help others beyond their finish line is where I have begun.

Transition is a common thread throughout life. There are small and large transitions throughout life's journey. Some are more challenging than others, but we could all use someone to relate to and learn from in these times. When you simply get started, other decisions, moves, and goals transpire. It is important to start with what motivates, drives, and inspires you. Find your motivators and then seek out how to trigger them. The noteworthy point here is to get started, no matter how modest the start might be.

What is a common driver for you in your everyday life? Analyze yourself a bit. Are you a problem solver, a teacher, a communicator, someone who loves to connect with people? I believe we have the ability to do our best work when we operate from our strengths.

Photo By: Mike Murray

Chapter 22

Transferable Skills: The Legacy Sport Leaves Behind

Since leaving a life in sport, I have spent a fair amount of time analyzing what transferable skills I have obtained. Having spent twelve years building a career in a field that seems (in my experience) to be quite untransferable, it is important for me to be able to articulate and express the strengths and skills I obtained in my time as an athlete. I have found myself feeling defensive at times, but deep down I know what I am made of. A sports career is so much more than the activity itself. It is a life journey that truly tests a person's physical, emotional, mental, as well as spiritual side. Transferable skills from sports that apply successfully to real life include, and are not limited to this impressive list:

- **Time management**: an ability to organize time—balancing a rigorous workload of full-time athletics, travel, school, family etc.
- **Team player**: an ability to work well with others—focusing often on team effort toward group goals to the sacrifice of ego and personal goals.
- **Leadership abilities**: an ability to lead a team through group effort by building team spirit.
- **Goal-orientation**: an ability to focus effort, sacrifice, and self-motivation toward achieving personal and team goals.
- **Competitiveness**: an ability to meet and overcome challenges—gaining insight from winning and losing, testing personal abilities, taking risks, fighting battles.
- **Confidence**: building self-confidence through a winning mindset, belief in self and team, often in high-pressure situations.
- **A strong work ethic of persistence and endurance**: building the belief that hard work and determination will pay off, persisting under adverse circumstances and sometimes pain or illness.
- **Discipline and responsibility**: an ability to commit strong effort to practise, work hard, and give maximum energy. Adhering to rules and guidelines, prioritizing tasks and responsibilities.
- **Loyalty and trust**: utilizing a willingness to support the team effort, trust oneself and the efforts of others, and build morale.
- **An ability to give and take criticism**: giving and receiving criticism in effective ways, learning from mistakes and moving forward, developing communication skills in speaking and listening.

- **Resilience, flexibility, and coachability**: exhibiting an ability to bounce back, learn from successes and failures, as well as from feedback, and to move to the next hurdle, dropping negative baggage along the way.

> Does past experience in a specific role really make for the best candidate when it comes to hiring someone new on a team?

This list is impressive and most people seem to know that an athletic journey would provide such skills. I think that many people would say that they see most if not all of these in my real-life behaviour. That being said, there has been a huge disconnect for me when it comes to the reality of my perceived reception in an interview. I have received push back and reluctance, because I do not have "experience." I am not talking about the experience required to practise medicine, for instance; I am talking about entry-level positions in retail. I know experience is a key component of the work world; it has come up in conversations all around me even when it was not for a job that I was applying, but even for the Lululemon job I left behind and the candidate who came after me.

Does past experience in a specific role really make for the best candidate when it comes to hiring someone new on a team?

I am very drained by feeling as though I am coming from a defensive place on this topic. I didn't start rowing until I was twenty-one, so I took the opportunity to have countless entry-level jobs from the time I was fifteen until I made the national team in 2006. It wasn't as though I lived on a lake somewhere with my head in the clouds. I then retired at thirty-three with a Bachelor of Arts in Criminology from Simon Fraser University in British Columbia, countless world stage medals in rowing, an Olympic silver medal, and participation in two Olympic Games. And I followed this up with top grades in a one-year fashion-merchandising diploma at Blanche Macdonald Centre in Vancouver, finished rowing, and returned to Vancouver.

All of this and I have been asked if I have retail experience multiple times when applying for entry-level positions and even some short-term unpaid internships! I understand that the easiest fit would be someone with experience in the role, but I feel I have so much to offer. By applying for and seeking entry-level positions, I was trying to open doors and learn new fields, but I felt rejected. I am not quite sure if I am missing something, but should I have been getting the message that if I had stayed back and folded T-shirts at The Gap, I would be better qualified to get work … even if the work were unpaid?

As you can imagine, I have had low moments after these encounters and I have felt underqualified and useless; but I've had to pick myself up and dust myself off reminding myself that regardless of how this experience made me feel, it is not the truth of who I am. A high-level athlete is someone to whom most people find it very hard to relate. I have found there to be many common questions, assumptions, and confusions when interacting with people outside the sports world, and even outside the rowing world, to dial the specialty even further. Many professional individuals in niches can likely relate, for instance, parents, scientists, and servers. When I was spending the majority of my time doing something with others who are doing that same thing, I only felt genuinely understood by those who shared my time: the inside jokes, the shared agonies, defeats, and successes.

I have been told that it takes someone who "gets it" to give me a job opportunity. Always look for those people. It goes back to surrounding myself with people who live in a world of possibility and acknowledge what I bring to the table. Those people are out there. The stronger my vision gets for my future, the easier it has been for people to jump on board and understand how our relationship could be mutually beneficial.

Photo By: Dawna Guloien

Chapter 23

Building a Tribe

Building a tribe of people who will support you and uplift your spirits is definitely important in moving forward. Finding your new passion and being successful requires building a network of solid people around you, whether you pay them or not. Through this transition journey, it has dawned on me and humbled me to have it reinforced that it takes a tribe to be successful. No successful journey is marched alone. This is a lesson I learned in rowing, but I forgot it in the initial stage of my life beyond rowing.

If you cannot provide something for yourself that you need, then why wouldn't you invest in paying for that service? Personal training is a big example to which most people can relate. Sometimes, all it takes for you to get yourself to the gym is putting the money down and making an appointment. For me, I am big on group fitness classes for this reason. Most only give you a twelve-hour window to cancel and paying that penalty combined with making the commitment is solid incentive to ensure I will show up.

A lot of athletes go into public speaking and coaching. I think both can be great options. I have been drawn to public speaking and sharing my story to help people, and I'm also drawn to analyze different topics for others. I can be extroverted and outgoing, but I can also be shy and introverted. In my initial speaking events, I felt utterly drained and exhausted after putting myself in front of a crowd. I had also struggled to prepare my speech and was left feeling unprepared. Public speaking is a craft that takes time to harness and develop. As I naively thought in the beginning, I could just force it to happen overnight. It takes time and, therefore, patience. There's that "patience" word again.

My ability to navigate successfully through this part of my journey can be attributed to the large tribe around me. I lean on a tribe of individuals who have helped to inspire and empower me to go after whatever it is that I want. Whether it is the seemingly simple task of getting out of the house for a coffee or the bigger life goal of dialling in my future career pursuits, each member of my tribe has helped me work toward the bigger picture: a successful, self-sustainable, happy existence!

The people that you choose to surround yourself with are key. In times of transition, there are crucial people to align with—your family and friends are the ones who know you best, so they are a great starting point. Teammates and other individuals from your athletic career could be great people to understand you; because they have walked in your shoes, they can provide the most comfort in hard times. I know that every time I hang out with my teammates or talk with them on the phone, I am always pleasantly surprised to hear a mirror image of my feelings and opinions because we share so much of the same perspective.

Next would be those individuals whom you might pay—sports psychologists, more general psychologists and counsellors, doctors, nutritionists, personal trainers, career counsellors, speaking coaches, publishers, and mentors.

> Rather than trying to white knuckle it on your own, fight the urge to seclude yourself, because no good comes of being alone for too long.

Don't hole up in your apartment and hide from other humans. On some days, it seems like such a great idea. I raced Samsung World Rowing Cup I in Sydney, Australia in March 2013, the year after my Olympic final. Leading up to that world cup, I was able to train on my own and in my hometown. I started volunteering and joined my local CrossFit gym. I also spent quality time with my two sisters and my mom and dad.

Rather than trying to white knuckle it on your own, fight the urge to seclude yourself, because no good comes of being alone for too long.

There were moments I found myself staring at the wall. I was not doing anything and I didn't want to do anything. The lack of a purpose built up and got in my head. For me, getting out of that mode and creating moments outside my room, also referred to as "my cave," were helpful. Going for coffee with friends, walking the dogs, and attending events were my favourite options. Any and all of these options led to far more opportunities than getting trapped in my self-doubting, identity-struggling mind alone.

It might sound a bit silly, but one of my biggest social moves forward was getting my dogs. My first was a Yorkshire Terrier I named Charlie; then about a year later I got her brother Arthur, a French Bulldog. Although it is a bit crazy to take care of two dogs by myself, they really have been my at-home, support system. They keep me moving and get me outside when I might otherwise choose to stay in and hibernate. They accept me and love me unconditionally no matter what kind of day I am having. They really have brought so much joy to my life. They constantly make me smile and laugh, and if you have seen my Instagram account, you would know that they are totally spoiled.

They have also helped me see beyond myself in caring for another form of life. I have heard people say that dogs are "just" dogs, but to me they are my family. The additional responsibility has been a lot to juggle at times, but I enjoy nurturing them. I think they have made every day more fun and although I am a bit of a dog lady, these little fur creatures have grounded me and reminded me how to enjoy life again. They motivate me to get out and to laugh while playing tug-o-war. They are constantly snuggling up to me and giving me kisses; they are always up for a walk; and every time I walk through the door they act as if it has been ages since they saw me last. We have a special connection that I could never have explored while I was training and I am so thankful that I went ahead and added them to my life post-rowing.

Chapter 24

Transition Like a Champion

If I could go back in time and chat with myself before I decided to retire from rowing, I would tell myself to be patient and take time for self-reflection before pursuing anything. If you aren't confident of what your next life's calling is, know that finding it will happen over time in an organic way. You can try to force it or make it happen, but it then ends up feeling more frustrating and hopeless than anything else. I discussed this with a former high-level professional dancer who said she felt like the ball in a pinball machine after she retired, bouncing from one thing to the next, trying to find her next "home." She hated it. Being an athlete is a full-time pursuit. Others will acknowledge the time it takes to move on to the next thing, but most importantly we must recognize the significance of this contribution and understand that when that time commitment frees up, it doesn't fill up overnight as we might think.

Your Identity Will Be Challenged

It is important to recognize that transition is hard and it will challenge your sense of identity. I was naive (perhaps I was being hopeful) to think that it wouldn't take time for me to climb the next mountain, even though I didn't have my sights set on what that mountain would be. Pre-retirement, I looked back and would often reflect on the fact that I stumbled upon rowing. So, I had faith that my next big life goal would come along in the same fashion, sort of sneaking up on me. I still believe this, but what I didn't prepare for was the length of time that it could take. It is years, rather than weeks or months.

> My advice would be to think big picture, relax into life's journey, and embrace that you might never find another "rowing," and that is okay.

Even as busy as I am now with other projects, I still feel as though I am redefining myself. When I was so focused on my sport, I was in a bubble in which time became so dependent on my sport goals that I didn't notice time passing as part of the big picture of life. As I transition away from a season-to-season, or quadrennial-to-quadrennial approach, I have begun to see time and the evolution of self to be part of life versus a route to your next competition. They say life is short, but a sports career is much shorter.

My advice would be to think big picture, relax into life's

journey, and embrace that you might never find another "rowing," and that is okay. There is so much more to discover. The more you can plan for your after-sport retirement, the better. Preparation is helpful, but not the only answer. I believe life is an evolving journey and you can't always plan out every little thing. I believe I have used my perspective and knowledge from each step along the way to assist me in making decisions. Without this experience, I couldn't have mapped out my travels, nor could I have changed the outcome. This is, however, my outlook and not everyone will be comfortable with this notion. Planning ahead for your future by having an education, savings (I know this is not possible for most full-time Canadian amateur athletes), and a solid network is a great way to prepare and put yourself in the best possible scenario when you leave sport. In Canada, this is an evolving topic of discussion and there are resources athletes can access through their sport federations and Sport Canada.

Patience and Time

Anyone going through a big life change or transition needs to give himself or herself the space, time, and patience to work through their journey. Moving forward inherently means that something has been left behind and to leave something behind takes us out of our comfort zone. This can be horribly awkward and uncomfortable, but I have learned to accept it, bear down, and push on. This is the time when big personal growth and development will happen. This discomfort triggered my imagination and my inner strength, and it made me feel alive again. I whined during most of my lessons, but looking back I realize that pushing my limits, comfort zones, and personal barriers really helped me to grow and develop as a person. There is always the option to stay safe and comfortable, but that is not where the magic happens.

We have all heard the mantra, "Do something every day that scares you," but few people actually go out and do it. Each time we test ourselves, we move forward and progress.

Sharing my story and trying to help others through their transitions are scary for me, but I am not letting fear hold me back. I do not pursue this venture without having questions of myself and my abilities, questions such as, "Can I write a book? Will people receive my messages well?" I am not exempt from personal doubt, no one is; but in order to progress we must ignore these unhelpful fears and forge ahead toward whatever it is we want.

When I finished my rowing career, I think part of me thought that I was going to shift into a more "normal" life and existence. Now my perspective on this idea of "normal" has shifted. I am not sure there is such a thing as normal and I am okay with that. I see normal as safe and conventional and, although that can be positive, I have had really great experiences being abnormal, unconventional, and unsafe in my pursuit of a big dream. I have an Olympic silver medal and a rare life experience.

Transition is part of the journey and it is not going to happen overnight. I remember hearing that it would take five years to feel "normal" again, and although I heard that, I didn't get it. I still wanted and believed that things would evolve and happen and I would feel settled right away. When this didn't happen, I felt frustrated that things weren't going the way I thought they should. Time is the prescription hardest to embrace when you want something in the now, but it really is not only the best antidote, but it cannot be inauthentically altered. It is what it is. Hear it and let it sink in. It doesn't mean we don't move forward in the interim, and it doesn't mean that progress cannot be made right out of the gates. Think of the years it took to become an expert in your field. If you were to take on learning a new language tomorrow, would you expect to be fluent in a week?

Undeniably, there is a process to the transition. Regardless of your process and the individual circumstances you are working with, five years is a solid timeline to work toward and within. Don't panic now. Just because it takes five years does not mean that your life is on hold for five years. It is a timeline you can wrap your brain around. It is a long enough stretch that you will in some ways be forced to persevere through the frustrating moments when you feel you should be somewhere and you are not; you can recognize five years as a path you can allow yourself to travel.

> If you were to take on learning a new language tomorrow, would you expect to be fluent in a week?

Even when what you do with your time changes and as a result your identity changes, who you are at your core doesn't change. I use my inner Olympian every day. Being my best, always striving for more and never settling for less than my best when I am focused on the goal at hand is how I made every crew I rowed in. This is how I approach my life beyond rowing as well. It has taken some time for me to realize and accept this as an amazing muscle I developed over my journey. This is something I can help train and teach others so they can find their inner Olympian.

I sound so strong, as though I have it all figured out now, but I don't. I don't have all the answers and I still have bad days. My support system, which includes my family and friends, is key in reminding me to calm myself down and give myself the time to figure it all out. The people who know me have been instrumental in mirroring back to me what I am projecting. I share with them where my head is at and how I feel. Sometimes, they tell me I am being silly, sometimes they help with solutions, and sometimes they just listen. I feel lucky to have people like this in my life.

Sometimes just saying what you are thinking out loud is helpful because when you say it aloud and release your inner demons to another person, you give yourself the opportunity to really "hear" your thoughts differently. The feedback you receive is often what you would give yourself after hearing what you are feeling.

We will not all walk the same road, but our emotions during transition, change, and personal development are universal. We will all come across the same emotions and struggles, and we can help one another through sharing and empathizing with each other. It is important to remember that you are not alone and you are not the only one who struggles.

Your Feelings Are Normal

Feelings of depression and anxiety are normal; you are not going crazy. I have talked to other athletes and all have told me they understand the feelings I am talking about when I describe feeling lost, listless, sad, panicked, and unmotivated.

I can especially relate to these feelings and emotions, because I have always felt them. I have been a nervous person since childhood and I have struggled with anxiety since I can remember. I have managed to create a lifestyle and habits that help me to minimize what I would label "unhelpful emotional states." Routine in my life is one strategy to make me feel calm and in control of my emotions, and rowing was a huge part of my routine and stability. Finding rowing was how I learned that about myself and, moving forward, I have re-established a routine. I still eat oatmeal for breakfast, I still work out most days, and I have built-in obligations and timelines that I work towards. Without this routine, I feel lost.

This is a great opportunity to try new things and create a whole new world of structure in your life. Transition can be a wonderful opportunity for growth. In this time, we have the option to take with us the parts of ourselves that we most value and can use in the future, and make changes to the aspects that we would like to part ways with. Starting over is not a bad thing if you choose to see that it is a gift to have had such a great life experience from which to launch into the next. I loved rowing and I enjoyed representing my country and striving for excellence in the way that I did, but there were many elements of a rowing career that I really started to resent at the end. For example, I lived in Ontario when I was on the rowing team and my family is in British Columbia. I longed to be closer to them the entire time I was on the team. With my retirement, I could choose to live where I wanted to again.

I have also been asked many times if I miss rowing. I don't miss the rowing. What I miss the most is the camaraderie that I had with my teammates. I was part of a group of people who understood me and shared my passion. We shared our struggles and successes day to day and we belonged together. I was motivated and driven by the fact that we were dedicated to a pursuit bigger than any one individual. The ultimate goal was that we wanted to represent Canada in winning a gold medal. The intensity of our goal and the pressure we were under made that experience very raw and intimate in an emotional sense.

We spent so much time together that suddenly not having that built-in network day to day was my biggest loss and probably the part that I had mentally prepared for the least. The good news is that I will always have what I shared with them and they are now like family to me. I have been at teammates' weddings, snuggled with their babies, and brainstormed the future with them; and I always will. Just because the circumstances change and they are not in my everyday life, they, like family, will always be there for me and will always be a part of who I am today.

Short-Term Discomfort Leads to Long-Term Gains

When feelings of loss make you regret the change you've made in your life, remind yourself why you chose to make that change. It may be uncomfortable now, but this discomfort in the short term will lead to long-term gains. The world is your oyster and there is so much opportunity. In my most uncomfortable moments, I have wondered whether I should have stayed on the team until I got cut, rather than walk away on a high. These thoughts will feel extremely genuine and rational, but know that your doubts, fears, and grief are talking. If you share them out loud you will hear and undoubtedly see in a moment that these are fleeting thoughts that are unrealistic evaluations of your decision to make a change.

It was time for me to move on and in many ways to move upwards and onwards. I have goals to have a career outside my sport and I want to have a family. Having had a sport career later in my life, relatively speaking, I knew that I needed to make a change in order to move on with some other big goals I had brewing in my mind.

A great way to shift your thoughts and strengthen your mind in the process of transition is to think back to other times when you transitioned successfully or overcame challenges in transition. Realistic timeframes and expectations were likely traits of this past experience you remember; for example, learning a language.

Focus on Others

When you are going through anything, it can be easy to become hyper-focused on yourself, so make an effort to support others to get your mind off yourself. Helping people, connecting with people, and seeing the world outside your four walls can give you great perspective and help you remember that everyone struggles in their lives at times. It is helpful to have human connection in these times.

During my mom's second round of major spine surgeries, she shared a room with a man named Charlie. I never actually spoke to him, but I could hear some of what was going on through the curtain. He had recently become paralyzed from the neck down and was going through a transition that I would not wish on anyone. I could hear his nurse offering him different foods so as to give him options. I gained a different perspective through this small interaction. Charlie will forever need assistance to do the smallest of tasks that I take for granted. Something as simple as choosing yogurt before having a bran muffin would be in the hands of his caretaker and not determined by him. Charlie's energy was so positive and patient despite what some would see as a very grim circumstance.

There are people going through a lot out there. I do not mean to compare or trivialize transitioning from sport, because our individual lives and perspectives are relative to what we know. My point is that by extending yourself outward to help others, you can gain the perspective and strength you need to process your own circumstances.

Use Your Support System

Never forget how important your support system can be. Make an effort to keep in touch with your people and really talk to them and share your true feelings. It is also an option to go to a mental healthcare professional to whom you can open up and share your thoughts and feelings.

Circumstances will always be different, but the skills and attitudes required to be successful as you transition are the same. Stay positive, be patient, prepare, and be proactive in making the process as comfortable as it can be.

Strength in Vulnerability

My journey beyond the finish line has been filled with learning, experience, and progress. In moments when I feel like I am not doing enough and I am not where I feel I should be, I think about where I have been and what I have accomplished. Learning more about who I am and what I want out of life has given me a lot of perspective. My strength is in my ability to be vulnerable. It is not weakness to admit struggle. In admitting aloud to the people around me that I have struggled, I have freed up energy not only to be myself, but also to be my best. I have also opened up to the potential of helping others find their way and to be their best in the process.

Appendix

Quotable Quotes

Meeting new people and making connections have been critical to my development, especially as I have worked to rebrand myself and try to find my way.

Will I be able to speak to large groups of people and sound like a genuine version of myself?

We all doubt ourselves and only we can choose how we respond to our doubts.

Leading up to this moment, I had worried if there was such a thing as going too hard and ruining the race, but my body knew what to do. That first stroke calmed me.

What happens in the village stays in the village.

It is at this point that nothing could make us faster by large margins, but there are numerous distractions, mishaps, and errors that could make us slower.

I was present, but in a different way. My presence existed for one thing and one thing only—an Olympic gold.

The outstanding moments happen when athletes are fuelled by stowed emotion and energy and driven by heart and motivation to win.

As athletes, we put a lot of blood, sweat, and tears into our sports to have it all measured on one day, at one specific time, and in one place.

Like any pivotal life event we anticipate, it takes so much time and effort to get to it and then no matter how hard we try, it goes by way too fast.

Rowing is one of those sports that appears so calm and beautiful from the outside, but it is actually more screaming mad than tranquil inside.

I can attest that in order to repeat any successful performance at the highest level it takes a heck of a lot of hard work and concentration.

The journey from my first learn-to-row class to my Olympic final in London taught me so much about taking raw talent and becoming a great athlete with that talent.

There is no statistic for heart or team chemistry. There is so much more to a great athlete than his or her stats.

I would assure any and every upcoming rower that my success was due to much more than just the physical ability to crank on an oar and row backwards.

Potential is not a good measure of outcome.

Typically, the title of champion is given to the one who can push through adversity and insurmountable levels of pain, but that's a very simplified notion that inspires Hollywood films.

It is our imperfections and our struggles that teach us the most.

We all have internal battles, struggles, challenges, and areas we can improve. They are part of life and they can help to make us great.

Find a way to do what makes you inspired, engaged, and happy.

Whether or not I have an Olympic medal hidden away in my underwear drawer, I am still just me, a human, not a super hero.

What are you going to do now?

It is also okay to recognize the struggle, admit it is hard, and ask for help.

My greatest strengths ironically can also be my greatest weaknesses.

Coming off the Olympic high, I was running at high speed, ready for high performance. Even my Starbucks coffee could be served stronger! better! faster!

Surrounding myself with people who live in a land of possibility helps me to see and achieve the greatness I am capable of.

Coming together in peace to compete in a sport that we love is about so much more than the medals that are handed out at the end.

My journey was about so much more than rowing. It was about relationships, personal development, overcoming adversity, and performing beyond my imagination.

Sport taught me to think ahead, react without hesitation, and do everything the best I can as efficiently as I can with persistence and dedication, even when things get hard.

Sport taught me to dare to be great and in doing so how to be more vulnerable than I had ever had to be formerly.

When I try to explain my motivation for the sport, I answer the same thing because the answer has never changed. It was always about the people.

I am more than my achievements.

If it were my child who brought home a silver medal and did what I did, I would be endlessly proud. Why am I not as gentle and proud of myself as I would be with my child (who doesn't even exist yet)?

Transition is the human condition.

My stance is and will always be that I am not special or better than anyone else and I accomplished something extraordinary in spite of this. This to me means that anyone can.

I didn't know how to do athletic events for fun either.

It is best to set modest and attainable fitness goals and outperform. My lack of preparation forced me to relax, lower my expectations, and have fun with it.

The Olympic spirit is one of persistence, resilience, mental fortitude, determination, and adaptability.

Impatience with a side of relentless self-critiquing is a wicked combo.

I am not willing to settle. I don't want okay, enough, or mediocre.

That focus visible in the eyes of the athletes on television is pure presence and it has been trained and practised, as well as tested over time.

In a culture where we are endlessly critical of ourselves, we sometimes forget how great we are and what steps we have taken and the accomplishments that got us to where we are today.

I have also noticed that every self-doubt I fixate on has a positive and uplifting counterpart that I am usually missing.

Breaking down any goal into smaller, measurable pieces allows you to be present and focused on the moment versus looking too far down the road.

Writing a book, teaching spin, and public speaking in an effort to help others through my experiences are my new pursuits.

Appreciate what you have and never be afraid to go for the full glass.

The only way to avoid failure would be to avoid progress and I decided I can't do that, so I have to embrace it.

To anyone approaching this point in his or her transition, I would say you must embrace that you are going to feel a sense of loss no matter how hard you fight it.

Vulnerability is not always sexy.

Competitive sport is about staying focused and going as hard as you can physically muster, all the while showing no pain on the outside.

What stops time for you?

I am inspired to show up for others. This is something that I need to incorporate into my post-rowing life. "How can I make a living out of this motivation?"

Does past experience in a specific role really make for the best candidate when it comes to hiring someone new on a team?

Rather than trying to white knuckle it on your own, fight the urge to seclude yourself, because no good comes of being alone for too long.

My advice would be to think big picture, relax into life's journey, and embrace that you might never find another "rowing," and that is okay.

If you were to take on learning a new language tomorrow, would you expect to be fluent in a week?

Author Biography

Krista Guloien is a world-class athlete who achieved the pinnacle of athletic achievement by winning a silver medal for Canada in women's rowing at the 2012 Summer Olympics in London, England.

Her rowing career began as a student in 2001 when she joined a learn-to-row program at Simon Fraser University (SFU). Falling in love with the sport during her first practice, and inspired by other great Canadian rowers like Silken Laumann and Marnie McBean, Krista began working and dreaming toward the goal of rowing in the Olympics one day. Her quick rise through the ranks was nothing short of meteoric. After graduating from SFU, she moved to Ontario to train with Rowing Canada's National Team and competed in her first Olympics in 2008.

Known for her hard work, consistency, and boat feel—the innate sense of when the boat is in balance and going fast—Krista became a team leader who was valued and respected for her ability to push herself and encourage her team members at the same time. Her resilience and commitment paid off in August 2012, when she and her teammates competed in the women's eight and won a silver medal for Canada.

Krista stands out as a role model for young athletes and has volunteered countless hours to educate, coach, and mentor young athletes. She contributes her time to numerous community events and charitable causes, including Fast and Female, 60 Minute Kids' Club, Game Ready Fitness, viaSport, and KidSport. All are either provincial or national organizations dedicated to encouraging youth to lead more active and healthy lives by getting involved in sport.

Her achievements in rowing at the national level in World Rowing Cup Regattas, World Rowing Championships, and the Olympic Games rank Krista among the top female rowers in the history of Canadian rowing.

After the London Olympics, Krista settled back at her home in Vancouver. Through writing about her transition from high-level athlete to the next chapter in her life, she hopes to help others prepare and manage the transition from sport successfully. Since her time in sport, she has taken a one-year fashion merchandising program at Blanche Macdonald Centre, and worked at Lululemon in store and on the website. She now coaches youth, leads indoor cycling classes, and coordinates events for Fast and Female in British Columbia. Writing and speaking to share her journey, as well as motivate and help others in their journey, have become her full-time commitment.

She is passionate about helping people to feel empowered, confident, motivated, and worthy. She is also passionate about her family and her two dogs Charlie and Arthur.

Professional Speaker

In her book *Beyond the Finish Line: What Happens when the Endorphins Fade*, Krista Guloien shares her journey to the 2012 Summer Olympics rowing podium, as well as what came after. She is an author, speaker, spin instructor, workshop leader for youth, and entrepreneur who has learned first-hand what it takes to compete on the world stage, but also how to cope after leaving something behind.

As a speaker, she includes engaging stories, examples, and insights from her more-than-ten years of experience as a full-time amateur athlete. She has gained a solid repertoire of experiences living out her journey beyond the finish line.

Krista's dream is to inspire others to grow into their full potential, and to help people experience life's challenges and transitions like champions.

To learn more, please visit www.kristaguloien.com
To contact Krista Guloien, email her at kguloien@gmail.com

Twitter: @KristaGuloien
Instagram: kristaguloien

If you want to get on the path to becoming a published author with Influence Publishing please go to www.InfluencePublishing.com

Inspiring books that influence change

More information on our other titles and how to submit your own proposal can be found at www.InfluencePublishing.com

CPSIA information can be obtained
at www.ICGtesting.com
Printed in the USA
LVOW01s0534020616
490682LV00010B/50/P